Tithe; The Complete Thesis

Theologian/ Extra Curricular, Volume 1

Modise Tlharesagae

Published by Modise Tlharesagae, 2025.

While every precaution has been taken in the preparation of this book, the publisher assumes no responsibility for errors or omissions, or for damages resulting from the use of the information contained herein.

TITHE; THE COMPLETE THESIS

First edition. February 5, 2025.

Copyright © 2025 Modise Tlharesagae.

ISBN: 979-8230071525

Written by Modise Tlharesagae.

Table of Contents

Tithe; The Complete Thesis (Theologian/ Extra Curricular, #1) 1
Introduction 2
The Interest Is Worth More Than The Principle 9
The Church's Usual Mistake 15
The Principle Of Seed Time And Harvest 21
Dispersing Of Tithe In The Congregation 24
The Demands And The Dues 32
The Conclusive Interpretation Of Tithing 42
The Setman 50
Tithe 60
The Church's Usual Approach 69
A Tithe Of Tithes 74
The Abolished Tithes 88
Going Extra Curricular 98
The Three Tithes That Were Paid By Israel 108
With All Said And Done 120
Tithe: The Complete Thesis Questions 122

Introduction

Hello! And welcome to the theologian class.

This is the level where it is all told even beyond the way it is now; most abundantly. Herein you are about to be inebriated in matters beyond relevant to deeply induce you in to the former things as the current and the coming. It is not a study of Dues to the set reasoning of our dispensation but the amicable define and design of dues in all stratus and orders of humanity.

Showcasing the many forms seedtime and harvest has taken and elaborately indwelling the sphere of the twists and turns it has endured and suffered through the orders in time to be as we partake of it. There is no sparing you for later or separating solids with the liquids. Lactose one would say are longer dealt with and you are due for the unhindered attempt and triumph at breaking the bones of the word.

Hebrews 5:13-14 KJV *For every one that useth milk is unskilful in the word of righteousness: for he is a babe. But strong meat belongeth to them that are of full age, even those who by reason of use have their senses exercised to discern both good and evil.*

This is where we cast at you the bones of the word.

It is where you will be absolutely gnawing the bones of the truth to deepen wholly their knowledge of the evident truth about the dues. It is here where it might be a surprise to learn that unlike it has been commonly known. The seedtime and harvest principle does not just come from 430 years before the Law of Moses or the Old Testament and also that it was not started by man but God. The tithe of Abraham in **Genesis 14** is soon established as the first time man pays a tithe in the Holy Bible. That is to say, the principle of dues is older than even altars. Before there was a need to cry to God and even before there was a need to set an altar to lure God's attention to man. God before He was even in fellowship with man He set the principle of seedtime and harvest.

Man in his perfection in innocence was given only fruit and herbs with seed to saw back in to the ground for the expansion of the kingdom of God on earth. Before there was a need for an altar let alone even the blood of beasts to appease God. Man was given this responsibility and it was his only responsibility for getting a ripe and thriving garden.

Genesis 1:28-29 KJV *And God blessed them, and God said unto them, Be fruitful, and multiply, and replenish the earth, and subdue it: and have dominion over the fish of the sea, and over the fowl of the air, and over every living thing that* *moveth upon the earth. And God said, Behold, I have given you every herb bearing seed, which is upon the face of all the earth, and every tree, in the which is the fruit of a tree yielding seed; to you it shall be for meat.*

It does not surprise any now that all the other living things are given any other fruit and herbs; being the fruit and herbs that does not bear or carry seed within themselves. Thus they do eat but have to responsibility to saw back. So, there is no need to give them any form of seed for they have no use for it. Just man; has the responsibility to saw back and only what is food to him.

Genesis 1:30 KJV *And to every beast of the earth, and to every fowl of the air, and to every thing that creepeth upon the earth, wherein there is life, I have given every green herb for meat: and it was so.*

The principle of dues; one of the just simply done of ethics.

One would simply dismiss the **Dues Ethic** as the commonality of our faith. Thus making it available to and for any to partake of it as long as they have an income stream; regardless of the condition they live in or their status of salvation. Making it more like coming to church in our dispensation; it is a thing available and common to any and all. So, it is often or just treated as a means to come closer to church leadership and when one wants to climb up the church corporate ladder and has become the quick principle to fund the church and its activities. In simple terms many just do it because it is done in their church or denomination and because they are not schooled well enough in it or learned in its terms often missing out and carrying on later on keeping it.

Though if one comes to deeply understand it. They begin to know you cannot miss on it or just continue another time. It is what ties one to the decrees or declarations said upon a specific altar and what leaves out others though they are screaming hopefully to receive from the same altar. The principle has been reduced to the pathetic attempt by the pastor to rob the congregation by many. In doing it now and then when they managed; it often turns to be the little favor everyone does the pastor but in essence a lot is missed due to misunderstanding.

The Principle Of Dues or **the Principle of First Things** is one of the most enduring of Principles. After **The Principle Of Life** immediately comes the **Principle Of Dues**; for immediately after man's creation he is tasked to take care of Eden and his pay is announced. He must eat only herbs and fruit with seed; so he may **reinvest** the seed back in to the ground.

Genesis 1:29-30 KJV *And God said, Behold, I have given you every herb bearing seed, which is upon the face of all the earth, and every tree, in the which is the fruit of a tree yielding seed; to you it shall be for meat. And to every beast of the earth, and to every fowl of the air, and to every thing that creepeth upon the earth, wherein there is life, I have given every green herb for meat: and it was so.*

All the other living things are just given herbs and every green thing to eat but man was only allowed to eat herbs and fruit that have seed that can be put back in ground. It was not requested of all creation but only human; only fruit and herd yielding seed.

This key induction in to seed time and harvest being the reason why you are always taught that a Christian is like unto a man who has just inherited a field. In everything that comes through your hands there is a seed to be put back in to the soil or work of God. Also for every new thing there is a portion that by choice you render back to God; by your limit and standard. So **The Principle Of Dues** also unlike other principles it is not just about one set thing but two independent dues Christians must pay to tie their life and substance to the purpose of God in His servant of the house of God they are under. The often misinterpretation of tithe is that it is often called a due to God; but it is a due to the service granted the children of God by the hand of His servants. It was the introduction of the Levitical Priesthood that introduced tithe to the congregation of God: not the introduction of the Law of Moses.

In the most simple of ways. Imagine the principle of dues as a tax one pays to be a citizen of a kingship or nation. Not just a tax but a specific personnel tax. And think about what happens if the revenue services fail to collect tax in any nation. The administration and personnel of that nation would not be paid. So, take it and put it in to the kingdom of God. As the one who the due service is rendered to; is it appropriate by any means not to pay? Think of it not first about the church personnel. Think about first about the service you offer at work. If it would be paid spasmodically and anyhow when your boss feels like paying you. The derangement and misunderstandings it would cause in your house with your family and the school and the creditors. Then when tithe is not paid that is what happens in the house of God. His servants feel frustrated and deranged failing and uncertain at their service. Even in the early church Paul had to do decry the Corinthians for not replenishing his service for them. A thing that meant the tithe of tithes from other churches were being used to render them service.

2 Corinthians 11:7-10 KJV *Have I committed an offence in abasing myself that ye might be exalted, because I have preached to you the gospel of God freely? I robbed other churches, taking wages of them, to do you service. And when I was present with you, and wanted, I was chargeable to no man: for that which was lacking to me the brethren which came from Macedonia supplied: and in all things I have kept myself from being burdensome unto you, and so will I keep myself. As the truth of Christ is in me, no man shall stop me of this boasting in the regions of Achaia.*

The case of the above set of scripture tells a thing. The service of God has to be paid for! As Paul talks about how he is being paid by the churches in Macedonia and Achaia. Two areas that contain two of the most influential churches when it got to aiding Paul in the work of God. He does talk to the church at Philippi appreciating the communication they had with him in keeping up their dues even when not in the Macedonian coast.

Philippians 4:15-16 KJV *Now ye Philippians know also, that in the beginning of the gospel, when I departed from Macedonia, no church communicated with me as concerning giving and receiving, but ye only. For even in Thessalonica ye sent once and again unto my necessity.*

The simplistic ideal being as long as there is a need for one to stand upon the altar of God; they are consuming man hours. Meaning they are spending a vital thing that makes their life; time. If time is being spent for your service and aid; it means you are not technical or otherwise deserving to replenish it; but has to directly as it is being spent give the appropriate dues for it. Forget who is doing it. See it as going in to the government office for aid; it does not matter who helps you, it is someone who is engaged for the value of their time and their time has to be replenished by a due.

It takes an intricate delicacy to slice through precisely with the principles of God. A thing that needs one to be determined to study the word carefully and to grow in it and become an astounding exponent of God's will. Most would blame it on the new generation teachers that they do not take the newbie through it all, but at times the horse has to go down and drink; the word of God is a sure well of knowledge and it takes due dedication to drink of that well as it is mostly for the new testament believer riddled with figurines and much allegory. A thing that needs both time and affection to do take all the needed time to take in the word that is Christ.

A lot goes without being said when it comes to the principle of dues. The simple ideal being the name of the principle; a due is something that you are impending to pay at a set time for a set cause. So, your dues for the services of the kingdom of God is thus as urgent and timely as the due for any service or substance you attain by use. Simplistically most people owe God and are way way well overdue but they are still expecting to have the due services. It is in vain even now, as it was said to the saints of old.

Malachi 3:8-12 KJV *Will a man rob God? Yet ye have robbed me. But ye say, Wherein have we robbed thee? In tithes and offerings. Ye are cursed with a curse: for ye have robbed me, even this whole nation. Bring ye all the tithes into the storehouse, that there may be meat in mine house, and prove me now herewith, saith the LORD of hosts, if I will not open you the windows of heaven, and pour you out a blessing, that there shall not be room enough to receive it. And I will rebuke the devourer for your sakes, and he shall not destroy the fruits of your ground; neither shall your vine cast her fruit before the time in the field, saith the LORD of hosts. And all nations shall call you blessed: for ye shall be a delightsome land, saith the LORD of hosts.*

Then, if the same God is still in rule and He is still in the business of calling man to His duty. They are sure supposed to be provided for not by any form of cunning craftiness but by their simple dues. A thing that would not make any wag their head at God for the sufferings endured by His servants due to unpaid dues. Simplistically; when your due seats at home or it is unpaid. One should know it is someone's hard earned money and their child may miss a due opportunity due to not being deposited in the right place at the right time. As the Lord do call more to His service; may we the more follow Him according to the set principles; for He calls them know He has slotted them food at the due season.

Matthew 9:9 KJV *And as Jesus passed forth from thence, he saw a man, named Matthew, sitting at the receipt of custom: and he saith unto him, Follow me. And he arose, and followed him.*

Matthew 10:10 KJV *Nor scrip for your journey, neither two coats, neither shoes, nor yet staves: for the workman is worthy of his meat.*

He expects them to enter His service without bringing anything that is their own. For the one who serves the gospel must of necessity live by the gospel. A thing that means as the one soldering for any given kingdom they would be given to the work of God and have no substitute for it. It took the hands of Israel off the work of the tabernacle and put it on the shoulders of the sons of Levi. Meaning, unless for other means like praise and worship and other faculties according to he gifting of God; the man who partakes of the tithe should just aim for he work of God. A thing that even apostle Paul found at times difficult for he could not even exact wages of some churches of certain coasts because of their lacking character and lest he would hinder the move and work of God.

A thing that raises the eyebrow.

If they were fit to provide for the poor in Jerusalem they should have provided for him too. A thing that means their ways were shabby and were respecters of persons. As in did if it was fitting for Paul to serve them it was fitting for him to exact wages from them.

1 Corinthians 9:13-14 KJV *Do ye not know that they which minister about holy things live of the things of the temple? And they which wait at the altar are partakers with the altar? Even so hath the Lord ordained that they which preach the gospel should live of the gospel.*

Simplistically.

The servant of God should be a man who is done with world and warring for God. Like any other soldier who prepares and go to war. They war using the substance and the strategies of the kingdom of God. The separation and idealism of their value and work is so sensitive they were sent and told not to take anything from the backslidden of Israel. They were even told to only sleep where the incumbent is counted worthy by the city or town or village. To partake only of the things of that worthy house.

Matthew 10:5-16 KJV *These twelve Jesus sent forth, and commanded them, saying, Go not into the way of the Gentiles, and into any city of the Samaritans enter ye not: But go rather to the lost sheep of the house of Israel. And as ye go, preach, saying, The kingdom of heaven is at hand. Heal the sick, cleanse the lepers, raise the dead, cast out devils: freely ye have received, freely give. Provide neither gold, nor silver, nor brass in your purses, Nor scrip for your journey, neither two coats, neither shoes, nor yet staves: for the workman is worthy of his meat. And into whatsoever city or town ye shall enter, enquire who in it is worthy; and there abide till ye go thence. And when ye come into an house, salute it. And if the house be worthy, let your peace come upon it: but if it be not worthy, let your peace return to you. And whosoever shall not receive you, nor hear your words, when ye depart out of that house or city, shake off the dust of your feet. Verily I say unto you, It shall be more tolerable for the land of Sodom and Gomorrha in the day of judgment, than for that city. Behold, I send you forth as sheep in the midst of wolves: be ye therefore wise as serpents, and harmless as doves.*

Though it often happens in crusades and other soul winning efforts. We are not supposed to be chargeable to the lost but rather the saints of God.

Yet there is a thing though not common is found now and then among the children of God. One who is willing to serve their chosen career path and still he a pastoral member of the work of God. We say it is not fine according to the original order of Christ. For He said, you cannot have your hands on the plough and still look back. Compromise as an incentive as it happened to even the original great commission happen to many things. One would be surprised that the mandate to go and preach to eh world was not given to the whole church but only the eleven apostles; yet a change in order so the church actually bearing the young due to the persecution of the church. Where the apostles did hide in Jerusalem and the church first ran with the word establishing many pivotal churches that saw to the birth of the true works of Paul and Barnabas.

It is this slip in order that gave Paul the first result yeaning mission under Barnabas who was sent out by the apostles.

Dues Ethic: Perpetual Principle

The Interest Is Worth More Than The Principle

Why learn principle?

One would soon ask. The simplest answer is principle is the fuel the spiritual life runs on. Without a preordained order of how to do the sacraments and the order of worship approach would be often marred and unprincipled before God. And where there is no form of ethics, anything is permissible. Meaning in the absence of principle all things are fine before God and all. There would be no right and wrong and it would obviously be rife with confusion and chaos. A thing that would mean anything is fine and approach could be done in any way. But in principle we can precisely cut with the word of God as a finely designed and well sharpened sword. For when we understand specific principle we do understand their specific outcomes. Meaning whatever we do before God we are sure of our results.

Hebrews 4:12 KJV *For the word of God is quick, and powerful, and sharper than any twoedged sword, piercing even to the dividing asunder of soul and spirit, and of the joints and marrow, and is a discerner of the thoughts and intents of the heart.*

The word of God does not define self as a two-edged sword: but it defines self as sharper than a two-edged sword. The precision with which it divides when well handled is thus narrated to be so specific it would asunder soul and spirit and even thoughts from intents of the heart. These four being a thing beyond a physical measure do need something that can go beyond the natural in to the corporeal to yean results.

One familiar with the writings of Paul would often pick the early church in its infancy did not have any form of principle on how to take the Holy Communion. And Paul do narrate some did even drink to be stoned in church. Even did some of the church members bring humongous portions of bread just to show how well-off they are. A thing that did need a principle; a principle to give measure and to have a congruent Holy Communion. One that can loose measure of who we are or where we come from. For if bread is from a basket, and the drink from one bottle. None would compare to any and be wounded. Or else we mostly get lost in the chaos of our own hearts, as comparison would wear most out to even absconding just to avoid the shame of continuously bringing out the scrawny portions of breads.

While the lot do exhibit their best portions.

It is principle that did correct this thing. A thing that without doubt gave birth to returning to the original way. One loaf and one bottle and a scanty measure for all. Lest they be stoned and start being riotous. In the beginning the gentile church did not do it so, as it proves everyone brought their own portion to serve self as they pleased. And it also proves they did not even wait for each other but did gobble their lot almost ceremoniously at will.

1 Corinthians 11:23-34 KJV *For I have received of the Lord that which also I delivered unto you, That the Lord Jesus the same night in which he was betrayed took bread: And when he had given thanks, he brake it, and said, Take, eat: this is my body, which is broken for you: this do in remembrance of me. After the same manner also he took the cup, when he had supped, saying, This cup is the new testament in my blood: this do ye, as oft as ye drink it, in remembrance of me. For as often as ye eat this bread, and drink this cup, ye do shew the Lord's death till he come. Wherefore whosoever shall eat this bread, and drink this cup of the Lord, unworthily, shall be guilty of the body and blood of the Lord. But let a man examine himself, and so let him eat of that bread, and drink of that cup. For he that eateth and drinketh unworthily, eateth and drinketh damnation to himself, not discerning the Lord's body. For this cause many are weak and sickly among you, and many sleep. For if we would judge ourselves, we should not be judged. But when we are judged, we are chastened of the Lord, that we should not be condemned with the world. Wherefore, my brethren, when ye come together to eat, tarry one for another. And if any man hunger, let him eat at home; that ye come not together unto condemnation. And the rest will I set in order when I come.*

The words of Paul above do not just spell confusion. But also he says some are sick and some are dead because they partake of the Holy Communion against the principles he first gave them. Meaning though often not looked in to some can literally die because of the error we commit in principle. So, it is better to learn and know: before we even do partake or execute. Incase what we do carry extreme repercussions. It is not just in sacraments as above but also in committing any wrong. As apostle John do tell of a sin that leads to death; as did Jesus Christ.

Matthew 12:31 KJV *Wherefore I say unto you, All manner of sin and blasphemy shall be forgiven unto men: but the blasphemy against the Holy Ghost shall not be forgiven unto men.*

1 John 5:16-18 KJV *If any man see his brother sin a sin which is not unto death, he shall ask, and he shall give him life for them that sin not unto death. There is a sin unto death: I do not say that he shall pray for it. All unrighteousness is sin: and there is a sin not unto death. We know that whosoever is born of God sinneth not; but he that is begotten of God keepeth himself, and that wicked one toucheth him not.*

Principles are a simple watch dog to the heritage we own in the word of God. They are designed to make us prosper according to the designated doctrine in His word. Doctrine is a form of instruction built on a fashion form of the expected outcome and the designed working of the word in our lives by God. We would say doctrine is the compounded emotions of the love letters written vastly by God to us. And principles are the designed conscience to take care of the emotions that brings loving and submission to Him. So, the secret of a principle is not in its self but the interest it serves.

It helps us to not fall in to fashions or seasons of men but to be watchful of the seasons of God. It is just as it is now fashionable to curse and declare death over your enemies, it is an in thing now, but it is contrary to the word of God. So doctrine and principle preserve us from the doctrines of men and the contrary trends of self promotion and elevation. Principles are not just rules that keep us in the way of light, they all individually have a secret hidden within them. Their worth has more value than themselves. In every principle you have heard or know there is a deeper meaning than what simply meets the eye. A thing that needs much poring to understand and to be able to discern the importance of any given principle.

A Christian is like unto a man who has inherited a field. He has to continually take the soil to the laboratory to check its PH and "nutritional health", thus he needs to continually consult to keep a fit Christianity. He does not grow out of principle, doctrine or instruction or the soil lose its value after repeated use and his heritage diminishes. This book's purpose is to keep a constant reminder that we are as strong as our doctrine and we are as healthy as our keeping of the principles. We all in one way or the other need instruction and thus we need a place of consultation and a ready hand to dish it to us, but we should at first remember the Hebrew saying, that we do not just keep sound doctrine, principles or instruction, it is because the keeping of them carries a better end for us.

These words above are a sure counsel to the wise. That we should not just be keen to keep principles but rather we should understand that every principle carries an interest to preserve and prosper us. That is we should not just be keeping principles but develop an interest to understand what it means to keep them, for they all carry a hidden interest to those who keep them, and the interest is the most important and worthy thing. In short, for each and every principle you keep; you should not just know the principle by heart but should have a clear answer for your: why?

The understanding of that 'why?', should be so vivid you can with the easiest of ease eloquently pass it on. It should be specific and outlined to the core. Be it for reasons of salvation, faith, hope, maintenance, providence or spiritual growth; Apostle Peter says you must be armed with the reason: why? A thing fitting for the persistence needed and the soon found confounding ought of the desperation of maintaining our calling sure in Christ. So, if you do not know why, it might be for a reason you may not understand and end up messing things. In this one sure scripture the apostle says, one should be always armed to tell of the reason they do go through tribulation and do not weary out; it is for hope. But one has to know more about hope to do dignify their attribute for it would seem cruel of God to let us pass through those moments for now.

1 Peter 3:15-16 KJV *But sanctify the Lord God in your hearts: and be ready always to give an answer to every man that asketh you a reason of the hope that is in you with meekness and fear: Having a good conscience; that, whereas they speak evil of you, as of evildoers, they may be ashamed that falsely accuse your good conversation in Christ.*

This does not just go for our hope in Him. It goes with all principles we keep. Compulsory or mandatory to all, we should not in part but be fully aware as to why. It does not just go for principles only, it should be with all your Christian life. For you to say you are a member of any church, you should know its vision, mission and objectives by heart; and also the doctrine, because it is through the doctrine that you know what you believe in or what the church is founded upon. Not through the ministration or the church services, meaning you should get to know and interpret the doctrines of the church through the way you serve. They keep the outline of what you are in to being as a church. And it is them that defines whether you are a law or charismatic church, and so helps you conform to the God you serve. It is the principles that give your field all the pruning and the care it needs to grow and bear fruit. They help give God what belongs to God.

Mark 12:13-17 KJV *And they send unto him certain of the Pharisees and of the Herodians, to catch him in his words. And when they were come, they say unto him, Master, we know that thou art true, and carest for no man: for thou regardest not the person of men, but teachest the way of God in truth: Is it lawful to give tribute to Caesar, or not? Shall we give, or shall we not give? But he, knowing their hypocrisy, said unto them, Why tempt ye me? Bring me a penny, that I may see it. And they brought it. And he saith unto them, Whose is this image and superscription? And they said unto him, Caesar's. And Jesus answering said unto them, Render to Caesar the things that are Caesar's, and to God the things that are God's. And they marvelled at him.*

Principle do define, what belongs to God and what belongs to the world. It helps you distinguish between the two and help one stay on the strait path. All want to build security around their all, loved ones, property and their spiritual lives. In the old they just built a stone wall around their fields and cities and prayed to God for the rest. Even around their fields by principle they did have to erect stonewalls to do limit the beasts of the field from mowing their crops. For as they needed the mutton they also needed the cotton of the field and they had to coexist under their set and sure watch. To prosper and to mature in to a worthy produce both to dress and to feed our being.

PROVERBS 24:30-31 KJV *I went by the field of the slothful, and by the Vineyard of the man void of understanding; And, Lo, it was all grown over with thorns, and nettles had covered the face thereof, and the stone wall thereof was broken down.*

The above is as the Israel of old as the church age; a thing that also goes for the man who is praying to God. There shall always be the wise and the void of understanding. Praying to God has always carried a specific way. God had to take Moses to Jethro's house to train him in to a judge over Israel for a specific forty years. He had to be in the desert forty years to know it by heart and its highs and lows, so that he may earn the needed experience know how to navigate and be a sure guide for Israel through it. He had to be principled and indoctrinated in to the life of the desert before he could lead any through the desert. For Israel was to be baptized in to Him, and he was to be the commander in-chief of their journey to Canaan.

I CORINTHIANS 10:2 KJV *And were all baptized unto Moses in the cloud and in the sea;*

We are thus baptized in to Christ and HE is our commander in chief for our Christian journey. We thus should know not just how to wear the armor of God for our protection but also should know how to build a stone wall around our all. Even how to use the armor of God around us and to prosper in the Christian battle field. So the land we have acquired by our salvation, thus need not just the working, but the protection and prosperity and to know it we should look to who we have granted our lives. Israel granted their lives in to the hands of Moses the moment they walked out of the land they knew and the life they knew. They followed him in to the unknown, expectant that His God shall provide and protect them. A thing that did not just needed a God who can provide but also a skilled guide to lead to them to the promised land. He had adequately learned the technical know how of being in the desert and by being a persistent constant part of it. A thing that can prove instantly repercussive if one does not know the way of the desert or its order or design.

EPHESIANS 4:13 KJV *Till we all come in the unity of the faith, and of the knowledge of the Son of God, unto a perfect man, unto the measure of the stature of the fulness of Christ:*

So both the desire to know your God and to prosper and be able to maintain the blessings of God endowed upon you, should thus drive you to build self in to a mature Christian. Generally they say those who love cherries soon learn to climb, just as the wise says of the field of the slothful, I went by the field of the slothful, and by the vineyard of the man void of understanding; And, lo, it was all grown over with thorns, and nettles had covered the face thereof, and the stone wall thereof was broken down.

In Moses taking Israel out of Egypt, he had to have a technical know how of how to provide for them and guard them. That is why they had to sit down and listen to the law and its ordinances. So even us when we left our former lives, we became like babes in the hands of Christ. We thus have to consult his manual and get it interpreted for us by Him to how our designed lives ought to be. It is not easy to take instruction especially that there is usually a life that we formerly knew and has to adapt to the latter. For it is not just about adaptation but also about abandoning your people and their ways.

JOSHUA 24:2-3KJV *And Joshua said unto all the people, Thus saith The LORD God of Israel, Your fathers dwelt on The other side of the flood in old time, even Terah, the father of Abraham, and the father of Nachor: and they served other gods. And I took Your father Abraham from the other side of the Flood, and led him throughout all the land of Canaan, and multiplied his seed, and gave him Isaac.*

Though a thing of old, one can learn from it that Abraham had to quit his common heritage and leave his past ways to be schooled in the mandate of God. A thing that thus prove to us that for us to live in the promise of God we have to abandon our former ways by adhering to the design of our call to Him. We thus have to leave the lives we so well knew and come to a life we so have to learn afresh. A thing that means separating ourselves from former connections and allies and protections to run in to God.

Our promise is in principle and doctrine of Christianity. We thus have to live our former gods and stick to the new true living God just like Abraham did to prosper. God did not just ask of him to live the land and the people he knew, but also asked of him to be mature before Him, in order for God to prosper him.

GENESIS 17:1 KJV *And when Abram was ninety years old and nine, The LORD appeared to Abram, and said unto him, I am the Almighty God; walk before me, and be thou perfect.*

The word translated perfect, means mature or entire, is the Hebrew adjective: יָמָּת **tamiym** (annunciation: tawmeem'). Meaning for us to walk the blessed way, we thus need to be mature and complete before God. For the word of God says seek first the kingdom of God and its righteousness and the rest will be added unto you. A profound thing that means only if you know the kingdom mandate you qualify to get financed for it.

Matthew 6:33 KJV *But seek ye first the kingdom of God, and his righteousness; and all these things shall be added unto you.*

There are often more than a few things that people try before they can really trust in God or give up. People believe in power but do not always opt for the source. For Christ do say a profound thing in His doctrine. That providence and calm are not found in the laying on of hands or prayer or fasting, but in entering in by Him. Him being the door in to salvation, peace and providence. To enter in is to know the door and enter by it. The right door and you are well provided for. That is why we learn and learn even the more principle.

John 10:9 KJV *I am the door: by me if any man enter in, he shall be saved, and shall go in and out, and find pasture.*

The Church's Usual Mistake

The church's usual mistake.

The church's usual mistake is to think they own their tithe. As if they can give it to anyone who they choose to give it to. The tithe and first fruits are dues. Meaning it is your indebtedness to the service and work of God you get from a specific altar of God. In essence one has to be a sheep of a specific kraal. Meaning they have to be fully converted and set in a certain church fellowship to be deserving to be paying a tithe. A tithe except for the tithe of the kraal, wine and corn; is meant to pay church personnel: as any form of freewill offering is meant to build the church.

As for the said forms of tithe above; the tithe of the kraal, wine and corn; is meant to be eaten in the church so that the poor and the Levite among you may have food to eat and offers the widow, the needy among you, or of the church. Remember Christ most assuredly said it; there shall always be the poor among us. Meaning as you reach out for more and help up the many; there should be sure food in the store house of God.

It is not vice versa or upon the church board or the brethren to decide. When men were introduced to serve the altar of God; it was when the due hire was set for their pay in the congregation of God. A thing that means upon it all; one should be sure of their salvation and sure of their salvation experience to be termed liable to pay a tithe or give in any of their first things. You are prepared in a certain place and set well in to God in advance so that when you are well set in the vocation of your salvation you may be sure of the altar and the place that would declare you Christian; otherwise it is just a waste of your precious money.

In simple terms. It is the same altar that decrees you Christian that has the same power to decree you unchristian by another principle; **Christian Correction**. Otherwise the declaration should be seek and found by any who aspire to be saved. The baptismal experience should be from someone you can attest saved and sure of the way of God. Meaning there are only two who can decree you unchristian or Christian; the set man and the church. As it was given to Peter to do so individually as a set man of his time and the church as the body of Christ.

Matthew 18:15-20 KJV *Moreover if thy brother shall trespass against thee, go and tell him his fault between thee and him alone: if he shall hear thee, thou hast gained thy brother. But if he will not hear thee, then take with thee one or two more, that in the mouth of two or three witnesses every word may be established. And if he shall neglect to hear them, tell it unto the church: but if he neglect to hear the church, let him be unto thee as an heathen man and a publican. Verily I say unto you, Whatsoever ye shall bind on earth shall be bound in heaven: and whatsoever ye shall loose on earth shall be loosed in heaven. Again I say unto you, That if two of you shall agree on earth as touching any thing that they shall ask, it shall be* *done for them of my Father which is in heaven. For where two or three are gathered together in my name, there am I in the midst of them.*

Matthew 16:18-19 KJV *And I say also unto thee, That thou art Peter, and upon this rock I will build my church; and the gates of hell shall not prevail against it. And I will give unto thee the keys of the kingdom of heaven: and whatsoever thou shalt bind on earth shall be bound in heaven: and whatsoever thou shalt loose on earth shall be loosed in heaven.*

In simple terms. You should have a vision and mission of a set place where you function according to the mission and vision of that altar under a certain set man to say you are paying tithe. Or else you are casting your cash at ducks. When you pay dues; you must know it is to maintain a specific altar that speaks in your life. It is not to buy electricity or help a certain man of God or church. It is a due; meaning what you owe to a certain specific altar and mission and vision of God. Meaning the tithe is a due to the services you are receiving from a certain place. The simple ideal being of those who received help from Christ. They knew which specific altar to maintain; where they were delivered.

Luke 8:1-3 KJV *And it came to pass afterward, that he went throughout every city and village, preaching and shewing the glad tidings of the kingdom of God: and the twelve were with him, And certain women, which had been healed of evil spirits and infirmities, Mary called Magdalene, out of whom went seven devils, And Joanna the wife of Chuza Herod's steward, and Susanna, and many others, which ministered unto him of their substance.*

One real good thing one has to observe here is that though people are paying tithe or are providing for the gospel of Christ from their own pockets; they are not running Him. One common thing is when people begin to pay tithe they begin to run the church and even the board. One has to know the tithe is not their prerogative but a due. It does not matter the size or the amount; it is not yours but the due for God in your lot. It is what keeps the enemy's hand of your substance and even your beings and stock. It does not give you the right to be deciduous about the matters of the church or choose what it has to do. It is a due; period. Primarily someone's pay.

Let us say your tithe is like your monthly water bill. It is a due not your choice. Meaning from the standpipe that you have been drinking water, washing, bathing and drinking; that amount is summed up at the end of the month and you pay it or the tap is cut. It goes for your furnisher bill, your gas bill and your car bill; you give your car bill to the wrong motor company: the company that gave you the car will come and repossess it. It is a standard you pay for the service you get at the altar. And mind you if none led you to Christ or you do not have an altar you are permanently being served at: you are not in the kingdom of God no matter your class or greed.

So, find one and be part of the kraal; be a sheep. Christianity is not by one's rules but by Christian Principle.

The concerted ideal being the altar that serves you and maintains you is the one you must lay your tithe at the servant of God's feet in that place. In simple terms, if indeed tithe be a due; you owe your tithe. The reason it is called tithe it means it is what binds you to the altar. The word tithe comes from the Old English words teogothian and tēotha, which mean one-tenth. Being a calculative measure but has been apportioned by God to those serving fully His kingdom altars; meaning a thing that ties you to the grace of God in the place of your house of worship. Meaning you stop paying it you are loosed of the service of that house.

It is what you owe those who serve in that house permanently. And tenth of it is what you owe the set man of that place. Meaning the tenth of the tenth.

The second common mistake is to take tithe and start buying church equipment and even use it for church building and the sort. It is not meant for that and doing that is against the word of God. Tithe was not introduced in to the congregation of God for church building or service. It is and was introduced to maintain the church workers and the priesthood. These having leaked in to the New Testament they are sent and told to not carry a thing from their former life. The ideal being a worker is worthy of his wages.

Matthew 10:5-15 KJV *These twelve Jesus sent forth, and commanded them, saying, Go not into the way of the Gentiles, and into any city of the Samaritans enter ye not: But go rather to the lost sheep of the house of Israel. And as ye go, preach, saying, The kingdom of heaven is at hand. Heal the sick, cleanse the lepers, raise the dead, cast out devils: freely ye have received, freely give. Provide neither gold, nor silver, nor brass in your purses, Nor scrip for your journey, neither two coats, neither shoes, nor yet staves: for the workman is worthy of his meat. And into whatsoever city or town ye shall enter, enquire who in it is worthy; and there abide till ye go thence. And when ye come into an house, salute it. And if the house be worthy, let your peace come upon it: but if it be not worthy, let your peace return to you. And whosoever shall not receive you, nor hear your words, when ye depart out of that house or city, shake off the dust of your feet. Verily I say unto you, It shall be more tolerable for the land of Sodom and Gomorrha in the day of judgment, than for that city.*

Luke 8:1-3 KJV *And it came to pass afterward, that he went throughout every city and village, preaching and shewing the glad tidings of the kingdom of God: and the twelve were with him, And certain women, which had been healed of evil spirits and infirmities, Mary called Magdalene, out of whom went seven devils, And Joanna the wife of Chuza Herod's steward, and Susanna, and many others, which ministered unto him of their substance.*

The word with out much wavering shows that the work man for God has to be paid by those who He render service to. Even this has to have a standard. So that he may not over exhort and extort. Even Christ during His servitude had those who did provide for His altar to be sustained. Though He had no building or much substance for the work He did for it already took from much attendance of the Synagogues, He had those who did provide for His well being. It is not a new thing that apostle Paul says it also about a man who serves that he should live by the things of the gospel.

1 Corinthians 9:7-14 KJV *Who goeth a warfare any time at his own charges? Who planteth a vineyard, and eateth not of the fruit thereof? Or who feedeth a flock, and eateth not of the milk of the flock? Say I these things as a man? Or saith not the law the same also? For it is written in the law of Moses, Thou shalt not muzzle the mouth of the ox that treadeth out the corn. Doth God take care for oxen? Or saith he it altogether for our sakes? For our sakes, no doubt, this is written: that he that ploweth should plow in hope; and that he that thresheth in hope should be partaker of his hope. If we have sown unto you spiritual things, is it a great thing if we shall reap your carnal things? If others be partakers of this power over you, are not we rather? Nevertheless we have not used this power; but suffer all things, lest we should hinder the gospel of Christ. Do ye not know that they which minister about holy things live of the things of the temple? And they which wait at the altar are partakers with the altar? Even so hath the Lord ordained that they which preach the gospel should live of the gospel.*

1 Timothy 5:17-18 KJV *Let the elders that rule well be counted worthy of double honour, especially they who labour in the word and doctrine. For the scripture saith, Thou shalt not muzzle the ox that treadeth out the corn. And, The labourer is worthy of his reward.*

Though apostle Paul was liable to receive a tithe of tithes from the gentile churches he did not receive from some churches but received it from others. In simple terms he made comparison and did only exact it from those he thought worthy. The churches of Macedonia he did exact tithe and offerings from even to help the church at Jerusalem he did exact from them. A thing when he speaks to other congregations he does not say clearly, but to the Corinthians he told them; I have been exacting wages from other churches to do you service. Meaning though in the above letter to the Corinthians he says he takes no dues. If you read another letter for the same church at Corinth he tells them he is taking dues of other churches and he did thank the church at Phillip for continuing in paying their dues though diligently subtly said.

2 Corinthians 11:8-11 KJV *I robbed other churches, taking wages of them, to do you service. And when I was present with you, and wanted, I was chargeable to no man: for that which was lacking to me the brethren which came from Macedonia supplied: and in all things I have kept myself from being burdensome unto you, and so will I keep myself. As the truth of Christ is in me, no man shall stop me of this boasting in the regions of Achaia. Wherefore? Because I love you not? God knoweth.*

Unlike the churches of Macedonia and Achaia the churches of the region of Corinth he did not take a thing from them. Yet he commend and put to note the forth coming attitude of the Macedonian church when it comes to their dues. The above words also destroys the usual conversation that Paul did not take tithe or the apostles. It is a myth and a legend among talebearers; but in truth as in **2 Corinthians 11:8** he boldly confesses he has been taking wages from the church. Mind you: he does not say offering; but wages. Meaning he has been given an outlined pay, as means from the dues of the churches not just one but churches. Christ also though He left His service of being a carpenter did carry a bag. Judas played the crooked treasure of the dues given Him; not the money He worked for.

2 Corinthians 11:8 KJV *I robbed other churches, taking wages of them, to do you service.*

It means from the congregation at Corinth like certain other churches; Paul deliberately did not take anything by any means from them by any means for any reason. He did not want to be chargeable to them. As he professes to them as mentioned before. It was a choice because he did not deem the money from those worthy. According to their ways and approach not because he could not take it; but because it was not in the wholeness of truth that it would be ushered to him. So, he chose to wait until the right time; evident maturity.

Paul elaborately says it that even though they should as Cephas and his party did partake of the dues of the church of the Jews; they should have of the gentile church. Yet because they see it would somehow impede or hinder the spreading of the gospel; they of choice did withdraw or refrain from it for the said reason. Not that they do not want to exact the dues but because it seemed a peril at that moment to exact the money from certain churches. Especially the Corinthians who seemed too prone and susceptible to sin and debauchery. Commiting sins worse than of the unsaved masses.

1 Corinthians 5:1-2 KJV *It is reported commonly that there is fornication among you, and such fornication as is not so much as named among the Gentiles, that one should have his father's wife. And ye are puffed up, and have not rather mourned, that he that hath done this deed might be taken away from among you.*

1 Corinthians 9:12 KJV *If others be partakers of this power over you, are not we rather? Nevertheless we have not used this power; but suffer all things, lest we should hinder the gospel of Christ.*

Philippians 4:15-19 KJV *Now ye Philippians know also, that in the beginning of the gospel, when I departed from Macedonia, no church communicated with me as concerning giving and receiving, but ye only. For even in Thessalonica ye sent once and again unto my necessity. Not because I desire a gift: but I desire fruit that may abound to your account. But I have all, and abound: I am full, having received of Epaphroditus the things which were sent from you, an odour of a sweet smell, a sacrifice acceptable, wellpleasing to God. But my God shall supply all your need according to his riches in glory by Christ Jesus.*

So the payment of the church worker is the due diligence as Paul connotes it is born of Christ as Christ Himself said the work man is worthy of His meat. They did not work in the Synagogues of the time. Tithe was being exacted from the congregants but they had to exact from those who housed them according to the providence needed at the time.

Understanding that the share of our income that is tithe is not ours would also being the zeal to do pass it on to the right person the instant we receive it. Understanding though it labeled the share of God, it is what God uses also to pay His servants. If God makes sure you get paid in time, you need to be sure that His servants get their dues at the right possible time. A thing that means whenever you are called a child of God, you are shouldered with the responsibility to make sure someone is paid well in time and you will also get the benefit from your dues.

The church often makes the mistake to think they will pay when it is relevant for them. It is not upon you to do so when you feel like it. It is a due, the set date is day you receive it. That is why the dues are the only ace where God does not forgive; you redeem them. It means if you abscond someone's child might be cast out of school or someone be locked out of their rented house because you withheld or delayed their due pay. If you are paid well and well in time; you need to do so to God too well in time. It might mean the key to someone life or death or freedom; because they serve at the altar and it is from the altar that they must get their due pay in due time.

There are bills for those who serve too.

They are not maintained nor do they eat holiness. They are human and are to be maintained the right way as Paul says: *Who goeth a warfare any time at his own charges? Who planteth a vineyard, and eateth not of the fruit thereof? Or who feedeth a flock, and eateth not of the milk of the flock? Say I these things as a man? Or saith not the law the same also?*

1 Corinthians 9:7-8 KJV *Who goeth a warfare any time at his own charges? Who planteth a vineyard, and eateth not of the fruit thereof? Or who feedeth a flock, and eateth not of the milk of the flock? Say I these things as a man? Or saith not the law the same also?*

So, the tithe does not belong to you, unless you serve fully at the altar. Then if you serve fully at the altar, it means in the dues is your life portion. The dues are not for the church building or to buy speakers or church disco lights. The dues are for those who serve at the altar and period. Using them anywhere else is not just sinful but pure ludicrous.

.

The Principle Of Seed Time And Harvest

Seed Time And Harvest is a perpetual principle.

Perpetual principle meaning it is not governed or changed by neither covenant nor order. In simple terms it shall stand until the end of time. For it is said so about it in the word of God. The Lord said to Noah; while the earth remains or as long as the earth exists in the current system of things; there shall be seedtime and harvest. Meaning as long as there is sowing there shall be reaping. I know the ideal of harvest not being attached to a timing means it is solely governed by sowing or seed time. This ideal makes the principle neither Christian nor Judaic both faiths found it existent and shall leave it existent until the pulling or burning down of the system of things as we know them.

Genesis 8:20-22 KJV *And Noah builded an altar unto the LORD; and took of every clean beast, and of every clean fowl, and offered burnt offerings on the altar. And the LORD smelled a sweet savour; and the LORD said in his heart, I will not again curse the ground any more for man's sake; for the imagination of man's heart is evil from his youth; neither will I again smite any more every thing living, as I have done.* **While the earth remaineth, seedtime and harvest**, *and cold and heat, and summer and winter, and day and night shall not cease.*

The principle of seedtime and harvest like many earlier than the first testament principles are just specific sayings direct from God's mouth. Unlike the Christianity born principles they are not weaved in a recourse of allegory; but are just clear deliberate sayings from the mouth of God. It proves from its history or the history of the words that even when Noah was giving burnt offering to the Lord. The Lord did discern the imperfection of Noah but also was delighted in his desire to please Him. The Holy Bible clearly narrates; *And the LORD smelled a sweet savour; and the LORD said in his heart, I will not again curse the ground any more for man's sake; for the imagination of man's heart is evil from his youth; neither will I again smite any more every thing living, as I have done.*

In The Beginning

The principle of seedtime and harvest did not begin after the flood. It was from the beginning of man. It does not begin with man reaching for God or giving to God; but rather it begins with God giving man not just seed; but ripe fruits and herbs so that he may sow the seed from there back in to the ground of God or the Garden of Eden.

It started way before the inception of altars and even before human built sanctuaries. Before there was enough humans to make a congregation in the early beginnings before there was a need to cry to God or even the need for clothing or shelter. When man still communed with God face to face as it was in the beginning. God gave man a mature garden with a harvest due, and He tells him to eat only herbs and fruit with seed insinuating a need for sowing.

The seed

The seed being a means to sow back in to the process of security and growth. Man before he could multiply he had to have a way to sow back in to the soil so that he may be able to sustain and multiply the more still the more being satisfied by the produce of the ground.

The very first literal gift God gives man is stuff to eat; herb and fruit yielding seed. Meaning in God's thought process; providence and a means to satiate should come before the actual increase and multiplication of dependents becoming manifest. In God's plan it does not fall out of place before God can provide; or man has to beg. It is just like the promise of salvation; that whoever enters by the door shall find pasture.

John 10:9 KJV *I am the door: by me if any man enter in, he shall be saved, and shall go in and out, and find pasture.*

So, it does not begin with the New Testament believer; He handed Adam and Eve the garden bearing seed for the sowing and bread for the eating. Instead of sending them forth to fend for self; He pre-provided a plan to sustain and to increase the government of God on earth; bread for the eater and seed for the sowing. Before the rain according to Isaiah rained from above; while a mist did water the earth; God did give them the fruit so they may takeout of it seeds to sow for further harvest and expansion.

Isaiah 55:10-11 KJV *For as the rain cometh down, and the snow from heaven, and returneth not thither, but watereth the earth, and maketh it bring forth and bud, that it may give seed to the sower, and bread to the eater: So shall my word be that goeth forth out of my mouth: it shall not return unto me void, but it shall accomplish that which I please, and it shall prosper in the thing whereto I sent it.*

Genesis 1:29 KJV *And God said, Behold, I have given you every herb bearing seed, which is upon the face of all the earth, and every tree, in the which is the fruit of a tree yielding seed; to you it shall be for meat.*

The first things did originate with Adam's family. Being the seed of the fruits and herbs reaped from the ripe garden as given by God. There were no sanctuaries nor congregations but just fellowship between Adam, Eve and God. There was no need for further elaborations or narrations as there was no need for buildings or protection from the weather; as rain did not yet fall from above. The design of the rain that falls from above is a measure of punishment and the soon riotous weather. It is not of God's original design. Originally a mist rose from the rivers and watered the earth.

Genesis 2:4-6 KJV *These are the generations of the heavens and of the earth when they were created, in the day that the LORD God made the earth and the heavens, And every plant of the field before it was in the earth, and every herb of the field before it grew: for the LORD God had not caused it to rain upon the earth, and there was not a man to till the ground. But there went up a mist from the earth, and watered the whole face of the ground.*

After the fall when they had to divide self by enterprise. The first and second sons of Adam had to bring before God their first things. It is the first things of Abel that caused him to be killed by his brother because they were accepted by God. Meaning Cain did not do his best in bringing his first things and instead of correcting self even after being warned. He did not work at raising his bar he rather did work a way to fail the one who is doing right.

Genesis 4:3-8 KJV *And in process of time it came to pass, that Cain brought of the fruit of the ground an offering unto the LORD. And Abel, he also brought of the firstlings of his flock and of the fat thereof. And the LORD had respect unto Abel and to his offering: But unto Cain and to his offering he had not respect. And Cain was very wroth, and his countenance fell. And the LORD said unto Cain, Why art thou wroth? And why is thy countenance fallen? If thou doest well, shalt thou not be accepted? And if thou doest not well, sin lieth at the door. And unto thee shall be his desire, and thou shalt rule over him. And Cain talked with Abel his brother: and it came to pass, when they were in the field, that Cain rose up against Abel his brother, and slew him.*

It was the bringing of the firstlings or the first things or the first fruits of the flock of Abel that God was pleased. He did even pre-warn Cain to not be wroth because he did not meet the mark.

So, it is on the understanding of the enemy that if we do well before God we will be pleasing and favored by Him. So he has ever since been at it fighting the man who would try to gladly service the altar of God as did Abel. The enemy keeps rising Cains as in pride and prejudice. The ideal that a priest had to be introduced between man and God does not change the emphasis that the first things as means dues and first fruits are dues to God.

Dispersing Of Tithe In The Congregation

It would not begin or go without saying it.

Tithe cannot be pardoned so they are rather redeemed. Since of old time it would not be let to pass by prayer of repentance or otherwise but rather were redeemed and still where missed must be redeemed. Meaning starting tithing should not be a thing that should be lightly esteemed as there is a demand set that once began one cannot slack nor abscond. As with any other due as in house bills or levies the accrued ought is expected instead of being overlooked to be paid with interest.

So, anyone who is interested in starting tithing should be pre-warned and prepped for the long haul. As it would mean if they are not paid interest would keep accruing with the more unpaid months or years. As with all other holy things; a fifth of their value was expected then to redeem them when they were brought late upon the owed amount. Simply meaning instead of a tenth a twelfth part would be expected upon the continuance of the expected dues. In simple terms you are expected to bring what you owe with two percent more; of your income value or a fifth part of the actual amount of the tithe owed. Simply out a fifth of the tithe value.

Leviticus 27:30-31 KJV *And all the tithe of the land, whether of the seed of the land, or of the fruit of the tree, is the LORD'S: it is holy unto the LORD. And if a man will at all redeem ought of his tithes, he shall add thereto the fifth part thereof.*

INTRODUCTION OF DUES IN THE CONGREGATION

The introduction of tithe in the congregation of God.

Tithe was not introduced in to the church or even the congregation of God as means Israel by the introduction of the Old nor the New Covenant. It is a product of a need unlike a product of remorse as in the case of Abraham and Jacob. Rather tithe is introduced in to the congregation of God first by the rise and the inception of the Levitical Priesthood, meaning when God had to hire servants for His congregation He also had to work out a clear way for them to get paid.

The tenth is not made holy by the size or design but by the ideal that they are a due levy to God; being the seed that is on every fruit that you harvest and eat being in His kingdom. It is a simple due tax; not for furnishing the church or buying the church a car or children's church food. It is the hire of the servants of God; period. It is not just a hire for the services they provide for the church; but also an intricately divided hire for the servants according to their offices. Part of the tithe is also providence for the poor and the abiding stranger among the people. The tithe of the kraal, wine and corn is specifically set aside to do that. It is not to pay the servant of God but to provide food in the church of God and to always make sure there is enough in God's house for the needy and the tarrying servant.

Deuteronomy 12:5-7 KJV *But unto the place which the LORD your God shall choose out of all your tribes to put his name there, even unto his habitation shall ye seek, and thither thou shalt come: And thither ye shall bring your burnt offerings, and your sacrifices, and your tithes, and heave offerings of your hand, and your vows, and your freewill offerings, and the firstlings of your herds and of your flocks: And there ye shall eat before the LORD your God, and ye shall rejoice in all that ye put your hand unto, ye and your households, wherein the LORD thy God hath blessed thee.*

When God laments in the book of Malachi for Israel to bring a tithe to His house so that there may be food in His house; it is not for all the tithe of Israel but for tithe that is due to the poor and the widows. Being that Israel should bring to the house of God to eat and store the remainder in His house so the poor and widows may eat in His house. Otherwise, apart from the corn, wine and kraal tithes; the increase went to the Levitical Priesthood according to the measure and divide preordained by God.

Deuteronomy 14:22-29 KJV *Thou shalt truly tithe all the increase of thy seed, that the field bringeth forth year by year. And thou shalt eat before the LORD thy God, in the place which he shall choose to place his name there, the tithe of thy corn, of thy wine, and of thine oil, and the firstlings of thy herds and of thy flocks; that thou mayest learn to fear the LORD thy God always. And if the way be too long for thee, so that thou art not able to carry it; or if the place be too far from thee, which the LORD thy God shall choose to set his name there, when the LORD thy God hath blessed thee: Then shalt thou turn it into money, and bind up the money in thine hand, and shalt go unto the place which the LORD thy God shall choose: And thou shalt bestow that money for whatsoever thy soul lusteth after, for oxen, or for sheep, or for wine, or for strong drink, or for whatsoever thy soul desireth: and thou shalt eat there before the LORD thy God, and thou shalt rejoice, thou, and thine household, And the Levite that is within thy gates; thou shalt not forsake him; for he hath no part nor inheritance with thee. At the end of three years thou shalt bring forth all the tithe of thine increase the same year, and shalt lay it up within thy gates: And the Levite, (because he hath no part nor inheritance with thee,) and the stranger, and the fatherless, and the widow, which are within thy gates, shall come, and shall eat and be satisfied; that the LORD thy God may bless thee in all the work of thine hand which thou doest.*

When Israel rebelled because of the absence of Moses, it proved there was need of a system bigger and larger than Aaron. More dedicated and sure and the Levites proved they are that crop that God needed to stiffen the work ethic of Moses.

Exodus 32:26-29 KJV *Then Moses stood in the gate of the camp, and said, Who is on the LORD'S side? Let him come unto me. And all the sons of Levi gathered themselves together unto him. And he said unto them, Thus saith the LORD God of Israel, Put every man his sword by his side, and go in and out from gate to gate throughout the camp, and slay every man his brother, and every man his companion, and every man his neighbour. And the children of Levi did according to the word of Moses: and there fell of the people that day about three thousand men. For Moses had said, Consecrate yourselves to day to the LORD, even every man upon his son, and upon his brother; that he may bestow upon you a blessing this day.*

The Levites were first servants of God and then any other thing they chose to be. Meaning when God incorporated men for His service of the tabernacle He did introduce the price of a hireling with the duties of care of His house; and as long as there is a need for God to be served in these things. It would always mean men have to leave their all and follow God. A thing that was more practical in the times of Israel for they literally had to carry His temple about as the tent of meeting.

It did not die with the old Testament as Christ in His former glory did swear to continue after the order of Melchisedek or the Levitical Priesthood to choose shepherds though no longer by their father's house but by the choice of their hearts towards Him.

Jeremiah 3:15-19 KJV *And I will give you pastors according to mine heart, which shall feed you with knowledge and understanding. And it shall come to pass, when ye be multiplied and increased in the land, in those days, saith the LORD, they shall say no more, The ark of the covenant of the LORD: neither shall it come to mind: neither shall they remember it; neither shall they visit it; neither shall that be done any more. At that time they shall call Jerusalem the throne of the LORD; and all the nations shall be gathered unto it, to the name of the LORD, to Jerusalem: neither shall they walk any more after the imagination of their evil heart. In those days the house of Judah shall walk with the house of Israel, and they shall come together out of the land of the north to the land that I have given for an inheritance unto your fathers. But I said, How shall I put thee among the children, and give thee a pleasant land, a goodly heritage of the hosts of nations? And I said, Thou shalt call me, My father; and shalt not turn away from me.*

The Lord talks of a time when the faith of all people's shall be looking into Him and there shall no longer be an ark of Covenant which is our current system of believe. He says He shall chose shepherds according to His heart. A change of Order we see with inception of the gentile church where any can be raised to be bishop and even a deacon according to their love and desire for God's work. (Read **the Empty Office** by same author)

The continued need for the hirelings is what keeps the need for a levy to maintain them. Jesus does not just allow the choice based but also gives the four fold ministry as a gift to the church of God. They are in the hands of the church as gifts to work the wonders and tell the mysteries of God; as a gift given to the church. Meaning they are disposed to the church's usage for a hire to maintain them. They are not born or called to a personal purpose but to care nourish the church within and withal.

Ephesians 4:9-16 KJV *(Now that he ascended, what is it but that he also descended first into the lower parts of the earth? He that descended is the same also that ascended up far above all heavens, that he might fill all things.) And he gave some, apostles; and some, prophets; and some, evangelists; and some, pastors and teachers; For the perfecting of the saints, for the work of the ministry, for the edifying of the body of Christ: Till we all come in the unity of the faith, and of the knowledge of the Son of God, unto a perfect man, unto the measure of the stature of the fulness of Christ: That we henceforth be no more children, tossed to and fro, and carried about with every wind of doctrine, by the sleight of men, and cunning craftiness, whereby they lie in wait to deceive; But speaking the truth in love, may grow up into him in all things, which is the head, even Christ: From whom the whole body fitly joined together and compacted by that which every joint supplieth, according to the effectual working in the measure of every part, maketh increase of the body unto the edifying of itself in love.*

The personnel are the cause of the introduction and keeping of tithe in the church. Though part of the tithe is openly eaten and shared with the stranger and the poor being the tithe of the kraal. One can do surely tell, it is among the servants of the house of God that even the cry in Malachi calls for the tithe that comes to the store house of the Lord.

They were not originally in the plan of God. But when they did rise to the call when Moses did ask Israel to sanctify self for God they did accordingly by acknowledging their wrong institutionalizing and by rite introducing the need for a tithe in the congregation of God.

THE THREE SPECIFIC DIVIDENDS OF DUES IN A CONGREGATION

There are three specific uses of tithes in a congregational setting.

These three were from the beginning of introducing tithing set and those areas still remains as the need and the surfeiting is still done the old way.

The Tithe (Portion Of Pastor And The Church Worker)

The tithe of Israel was ascribed the Levites for inheritance as they had no state of their own among the sons of Jacob. They depended on getting a tithe from Israel as a means of attaining a harvest continually.

Numbers 18:21-24 KJV *And, behold, I have given the children of Levi all the tenth in Israel for an inheritance, for their service which they serve, even the service of the tabernacle of the congregation. Neither must the children of Israel henceforth come nigh the tabernacle of the congregation, lest they bear sin, and die. But the Levites shall do the service of the tabernacle of the congregation, and they shall bear their iniquity: it shall be a statute for ever throughout your generations, that among the children of Israel they have no inheritance. But the tithes of the children of Israel, which they offer as an heave offering unto the LORD, I have given to the Levites to inherit: therefore I have said unto them, Among the children of Israel they shall have no inheritance.*

One should look carefully that the work of the house of God is given to Levi. So, the tithe is due to him and the rest of the congregation can just go about their business and do the work of the congregation through them. A sound reminder of why a tithe is paid. We are in a season and a time when the church herself seems to be befallen by erroneous teaching and conduct in all ranks. Where the pastor is no longer the shepherd but the head of the house. It ought to be understood, a shepherd is not the head of the house. So, a shepherd cannot stand in the house of God and have the tile of God being Father or Daddy. Even the titles and names ascribed the pastor should not parallel of God. God is the Father of the house not the pastor.

Matthew 23:9 KJV *And call no man your father upon the earth: for one is your Father, which is in heaven.*

They are raised to serve God's house. Being servants to the Father of the house means you are not permanent but subject to the owner of the house and His responsible children. For when a heir is mature they become better than a servant.

Galatians 4:1-2 KJV *Now I say, That the heir, as long as he is a child, differeth nothing from a servant, though he be lord of all; But is under tutors and governors until the time appointed of the father.*

The Tithe Of Tithes (Portion Of The Setman)

The tithe of tithes is the portion of the overseer be it a bishop or otherwise; who ever oversees a set ministry or church under a sole vision is the one who takes the portion of the overseer. In the Old Testament the whole tithe of tithes of the nation of Israel was taken by Aaron.

Then the abiding lot was allotted the Levitical Priesthood.

Numbers 18:21, 24, 26-29 KJV *And, behold, I have given the children of Levi all the tenth in Israel for an inheritance, for their service which they serve, even the service of the tabernacle of the congregation. But the tithes of the children of Israel, which they offer as an heave offering unto the LORD, I have given to the Levites to inherit: therefore I have said unto them, Among the children of Israel they shall have no inheritance. Thus speak unto the Levites, and say unto them, When ye take of the children of Israel the tithes which I have given you from them for your inheritance, then ye shall offer up an heave offering of it for the LORD, even a tenth part of the tithe. And this your heave offering shall be reckoned unto you, as though it were the corn of the threshingfloor, and as the fulness of the winepress. Thus ye also shall offer an heave offering unto the LORD of all your tithes, which ye receive of the children of Israel; and ye shall give thereof the LORD'S heave offering to Aaron the priest. Out of all your gifts ye shall offer every heave offering of the LORD, of all the best thereof, even the hallowed part thereof out of it.*

It usually comes as a surprise that one percent of all the tithe of Israel went to one man Aaron. Meaning the Levites out of the tithe they received they received holy and unholy things; but only Aaron received only the holy things of the tithe by the means of a tithe of tithes.

He was spared the choicest of the things of the tithe of Israel. Being the Highpriest meant he exacted a tithe from the priests rather than directly from Israel. They brought and sought out the best things of the tithe unto him. Though they were not given heritage among Israel; they in form did have their own harvest out of the harvest of Israel and in turn had to do God the honors of paying the holy part too. Meaning it was a higher holy part; later in the book of Nehemiah named the tithe of tithes.

One other thing one would come to learn of Aaron is unlike the Levites having a little portion little by little among the children of Israel. Aaron's portion was the house of God and God was Himself was His lot. It is a sure thing that is definitely going to move people once they learn it has to be the portion of the set man; the ideal being in the current setting it would without doubt be deemed too much though a lot slotted the set man by God. It is one of those things that tells you even the children of God have a limiting agenda regarding the portion of the called of God. It is more of the place of the slothful and the one who gets the last of the baggage rather than a place of light showing the greatness of God. A thing that makes the struggle of the church evident and the promises of God farfetched. For if His high portion is not slotted the set man; then His eminence is misplaced in that house or place.

Numbers 18:20 BBE *And the Lord said to Aaron, You will have no heritage in their land, or any part among them; I am your part and your heritage among the children of Israel.*

Tithe Of The Kraal (Portion Of The Needy)

The tithe of the kraal or the kosher grazing animals.

The tithe of the kraal or the animal tithe (**Hebrew:** מַעְשַׂר בְּהֵמָה, "Ma'sar Behemah") is a commandment in the Old Testament requiring the sanctifying of a tithe of kosher grazing animals (cattle, sheep, and goats) to God, to be sacrificed as a Korban at the Temple in Jerusalem. A thing that means are in kind as the temple no longer stands in Jerusalem is a bountiful feasting on high day of tithe of the kraal because even then; vows and freewill offerings are given to fill and to abound the house of God. A thing that means meat for the Levite and the needy and the well among them. The ideal being in granting a korban, most of the meat is granted to friends and near and far of kin in the place.

Leviticus 27:31-32 KJV *And if a man will at all redeem ought of his tithes, he shall add thereto the fifth part thereof. And concerning the tithe of the herd, or of the flock, even of whatsoever passeth under the rod, the tenth shall be holy unto the LORD.*

The tithe of animals was not redeemable; and if one animal was exchanged for another both became sanctified. The method of levying the tithe of animals is indicated: they were counted singly; and every tenth one that passed under the rod became the tithe animal.

The high day that marked the beginning of the year of tithing was a define splendor. They fixed a particular day to mark the beginning of the year for tithing. The new year's day for the tithing of animals (**Rosh Hashanah L'Ma'sar Behemah**) was the day the tithe of the kraal came in on the high day when vows and free will offering were granted God. A thing that meant plenty days unto the congregation of God; but well and above all, it meant a continuous feast or providence to the widow, the fatherless and the needy among them.

Deuteronomy 14:22-29 KJV *Thou shalt truly tithe all the increase of thy seed, that the field bringeth forth year by year. And thou shalt eat before the LORD thy God, in the place which he shall choose to place his name there, the tithe of thy corn, of thy wine, and of thine oil, and the firstlings of thy herds and of thy flocks; that thou mayest learn to fear the LORD thy God always. And if the way be too long for thee, so that thou art not able to carry it; or if the place be too far from thee, which the LORD thy God shall choose to set his name there, when the LORD thy God hath blessed thee: Then shalt thou turn it into money, and bind up the money in thine hand, and shalt go unto the place which the LORD thy God shall choose: And thou shalt bestow that money for whatsoever thy soul lusteth after, for oxen, or for sheep, or for wine, or for strong drink,*

or for whatsoever thy soul desireth: and thou shalt eat there before the LORD thy God, and thou shalt rejoice, thou, and thine household, And the Levite that is within thy gates; thou shalt not forsake him; for he hath no part nor inheritance with thee. At the end of three years thou shalt bring forth all the tithe of thine increase the same year, and shalt lay it up within thy gates: And the Levite, (because he hath no part nor inheritance with thee,) and the stranger, and the fatherless, and the widow, which are within thy gates, shall come, and shall eat and be satisfied; that the LORD thy God may bless thee in all the work of thine hand which thou doest.

The Demands And The Dues

The tithe simply said is what ties you to the altar of God that you are served from. Meaning it is a form of servicing or maintaining the altar that you are served from. Here bringing in two specifics;

1. Servicing the Altar
2. Demanding from an Altar

Servicing the altar

There is a thing that we often miss, not everyone who is in the house of God or who is before the altar of God receives the declarations or the given spiritual things of the said altar unless they service it. In simple terms, it is not the one who believe most or shout the loudest who receives from any given altar of God; but the one who by intricate understanding services the altar.

In simple terms, what you get in the spiritual does not resonate from the energy spent in prayer or otherwise but the ideal of understanding how to receive or protect your lot. Many would go days and nights praying and fasting for protection of their things instead of just tying them to the care of God by a tithe. Though much energy and time is spent; it is in vain. Before you even begin to talk about the use of the tithe in the church. One should analyze the use of tithe in their lives first.

Genesis 28:18-22 KJV *And Jacob rose up early in the morning, and took the stone that he had put for his pillows, and set it up for a pillar, and poured oil upon the top of it. And he called the name of that place Beth-el: but the name of that city was called Luz at the first. And Jacob vowed a vow, saying, If God will be with me, and will keep me in this way that I go, and will give me bread to eat, and raiment to put on, So that I come again to my father's house in peace; then shall the LORD be my God: And this stone, which I have set for a pillar, shall be God's house: and of all that thou shalt give me I will surely give the tenth unto thee.*

Deuteronomy 14:22 KJV *Thou shalt truly tithe all the increase of thy seed, that the field bringeth forth year by year.*

Deuteronomy 15:20 KJV *Thou shalt eat it before the LORD thy God year by year in the place which the LORD shall choose, thou and thy household.*

Malachi 3:8-12 KJV *Will a man rob God? Yet ye have robbed me. But ye say, Wherein have we robbed thee? In tithes and offerings. Ye are cursed with a curse: for ye have robbed me, even this whole nation. Bring ye all the tithes into the storehouse, that there may be meat in mine house, and prove me now herewith, saith the LORD of hosts, if I will not open you the windows of heaven, and pour you out a blessing, that there shall not be room enough to receive it. And I will rebuke the devourer for your sakes, and he shall not destroy the fruits of your ground; neither shall your vine cast her fruit before the time in the field, saith the LORD of hosts. And all nations shall call you blessed: for ye shall be a delightsome land, saith the LORD of hosts.*

One would say Jacob did challenge God to uphold his physicality and all his physical things until he reached again his father's house in peace. He did not say God was his God: but said if God fulfills, then God shall be his God. A thing that means a tithe sets a price before God that says all my things physical are in your hands. So, when the thief steals from you or your field does not bear fruit the questions is; Did you secure it all by tying it to the altar of God. The simple thing being these are things that helps you withal though your spirit and soul are saved and set for His glory the flesh is yet in the physical world where all needs to be secured from the ills and disparities of your kins and substance from evil. Your salvation does not secure them.

The words above then show a clear outline that many often breach. They would call their tenth holy and set aside for God but then end up eating what is set aside for the altar of God. A thing that would mean they eat a thing not ordained for their health; so they partake of it to their destruction and unnamed ills.

Though the instance of Abraham is a bit different from that of Jacob. Abraham did refuse any pay or thing from the kings of Sodom and its neighbors rather choosing to abstain from their stuff lest they say they enriched him. He of his own choice did after seeing the protection of God manifest in his life did pay a tithe. A thing that means, he saw the hand of God first protecting unlike Jacob. Then he chose to acknowledge Him for the protection. A thing that is usually different in the church of God, because when the salary rise people then begin to fail to pay. They get privileged now and then tithe no longer belongs to God; instead it becomes my tithe. A thing that happens if the tithe becomes a lump some of some sort. They begin to govern the church and expect to make and take decisions about its use and its function. A thing that often would make the deciduously determine it has to be spent in buying worthy things for the church. Instead of being wasted on being given to slothful men who has to go and work.

Whatever has been attained once grabbed one should rather focus on maintaining it. The way they captured it. With the right and same dues as before they had reached their goal; as when they have reached their goal. Lest they have to restart all over again. Abraham even after apprehending what he desired of God did see the need to not just maintain but to even start then though God had already accomplished it.

Genesis 14:18-20 KJV *And Melchizedek king of Salem brought forth bread and wine: and he was the priest of the most high God. And he blessed him, and said, Blessed be Abram of the most high God, possessor of heaven and earth: And blessed be the most high God, which hath delivered thine enemies into thy hand. And he gave him tithes of all.*

It is the thing that fails most that Abraham did. Unlike Jacob, God did victor for him first. Then he chose to maintain the altar or service it. Meaning he understood, if he could maintain what had just happened and secure that continuous favor in advance; it would mean the same favor would always flow in case of an attack. Yet most fail to learn from this wise decision, only trying to keep up when the enemy had already broken in.

Until the problems seem to magically melt away. The servant of God is usually hyper engaged men forget they are qualified for the job and so should obviously get it. They forget they have rights as children of God until apprehended. Once gotten; the old tale begins. When man begins to be secure and becomes family; they begin to know how much time the pastor and the workers of the church have just to kill. Instead they should be working for their own income.

Demanding From An Altar

Our tithe gives us the right to demand from an altar of God.

This simply means, if God said if you pay tithe He will protect your lot, then if you suffer loss you have a right to demand from the altar of God. Because of the agreement of a tithe between Jacob and God. Jacob did at times demand absurd of things from God like changing the birth colors of his uncle's flock so he may get the strong kids and lambs of the flock. Though arm bending God did always did follow his moves. A thing that made Laban even the more biased was not that he was a bad man, but the ideal that Jacob had always been a supplant and he was pinching him of all fat and good by forcing the favor of God.

He knew he had a deal with God and so he took advantage. Servicing the altar of God gives us that kind of advantage. It gives us the right to question God when all does not go well and when targets are not met. (For further reading; read **Introduction To Altars: Demanding From Altars** by same author)

Genesis 28:18-22 KJV *And Jacob rose up early in the morning, and took the stone that he had put for his pillows, and set it up for a pillar, and poured oil upon the top of it. And he called the name of that place Beth-el: but the name of that city was called Luz at the first. And Jacob vowed a vow, saying, If God will be with me, and will keep me in this way that I go, and will give me bread to eat, and raiment to put on, So that I come again to my father's house in peace; then shall the*

LORD be my God: And this stone, which I have set for a pillar, shall be God's house: and of all that thou shalt give me I will surely give the tenth unto thee.

There are things that often do get out of the way. Things that are not in the promises of God to His children. These things often happen to hinder the will of God for our lives and the only thing one has against them is the power to demand from the altar of God. The power to plead or demand from the blood of Jesus rallies in the initial strength of your servicing of the altar of God.

In simple terms, it is who you are before the altar of God that makes Him answerable when things are not going according to will at times. Jacob mostly on his part was toying with his uncle and demanded to break tradition that was not farfetched from the Hebrews traditions. He was simply into bending hands and that is what we usually call demanding from altars or being petty with God.

The Priest Of The Altar

Who is your priest and how or through who do you get His service and knowledge?

We all talk about being sons with Christ; but who gives us the know how and lead to the perfecting in our Lord God. In all simplism; who serves at our altar?

Ephesians 4:11-12 KJV *And he gave some, apostles; and some, prophets; and some, evangelists; and some, pastors and teachers; For the perfecting of the saints, for the work of the ministry, for the edifying of the body of Christ:*

The person or the people who serve at the altar are not mediators but facilitators between us and God. So, if you are to pay your dues for the service of God, it is in to the hand of the one who is perfecting you in to the image of the one you believe in. That is why in Christianity we have the five fold ministry who are termed a gift to the church of God. There are called a gift to the church of God because their lives have been given for the perfecting of the church, to grow it in to the fullness and perfection of Jesus Christ.

They are mandated to duplicate the total man in to the whole church. A thing that means a dedicated life time service at teaching people how to approach and be kept in God. How to maintain and service the altars of God in their lives. Whether it be family altars, altars of worship or service on their personal lives; it is chargeable to the priest of the altar of God or the set man to prepare and teach the church or congregation how to serve and maintain the altar of his and their God.

Ephesians 4:8-16 KJV *Wherefore he saith, When he ascended up on high, he led captivity captive, and gave gifts unto men. (Now that he ascended, what is it but that he also descended first into the lower parts of the earth? He that descended is the same also that ascended up far above all heavens, that he might fill all things.) And he gave some, apostles; and some, prophets; and some, evangelists; and some, pastors and teachers; For the perfecting of the saints, for the work of the ministry, for the edifying of the body of Christ: Till we all come in the unity of the faith, and of the knowledge of the Son of God, unto a perfect man, unto the measure of the stature of the fulness of Christ: That we henceforth be no more children, tossed to and fro, and carried about with every wind of doctrine, by the sleight of men, and cunning craftiness, whereby they lie in wait to deceive; But speaking the truth in love, may grow up into him in all things, which is the head, even Christ: From whom the whole body fitly joined together and compacted by that which every joint supplieth, according to the effectual working in the measure of every part, maketh increase of the body unto the edifying of itself in love.*

So, for the given life to the service of God. The first and due thing after Holiness is paying your dues.

Are you paying your dues?

Meaning, are you stealing the service of that altar or are you maintaining it?

Every declaration and every said prophecy from the altar of God does not take strength in your prayers or fasting. It takes strength in your ability to maintain that altar and making sure it is functional. Most people do miss this because they think power is by grace. The grace functions by hirelings, men and women who if they do not teach you or support you in your weak moment you would be otherwise naïve of the things of God. They eat real food and their kids go to real schools; that is the reality and that is why you left your place to seek God around them and to keep coming back to hear what they are saying. They are giving a service just like you give a service at your work place. Whether you know or not it would not permit or stop them from entering heaven. Yet for the price of their service there is a due that is set for you to pay being the tithe.

The tithe is not for church building nor for any other service but to maintain the personnel that keeps the altar of God. It is a portion of your life that is dedicated to pay for the service of God in your life. You receive any service from the servants of God; if it fails, do not blame the servant: first check if you are maintaining the dues for their service. You cannot steal from God; period.

1 Corinthians 9:3-11, 13-14 KJV *Mine answer to them that do examine me is this, Have we not power to eat and to drink? Have we not power to lead about a sister, a wife, as well as other apostles, and as the brethren of the Lord, and*

Cephas? Or I only and Barnabas, have not we power to forbear working? Who goeth a warfare any time at his own charges? Who planteth a vineyard, and eateth not of the fruit thereof? Or who feedeth a flock, and eateth not of the milk of the flock? Say I these things as a man? Or saith not the law the same also? For it is written in the law of Moses, Thou shalt not muzzle the mouth of the ox that treadeth out the corn. Doth God take care for oxen? Or saith he it altogether for our sakes? For our sakes, no doubt, this is written: that he that ploweth should plow in hope; and that he that thresheth in hope should be partaker of his hope. If we have sown unto you spiritual things, is it a great thing if we shall reap your carnal things? Do ye not know that they which minister about holy things live of the things of the temple? And they which wait at the altar are partakers with the altar? Even so hath the Lord ordained that they which preach the gospel should live of the gospel.

The above words of apostle Paul are usually confused with the ideal of not taking any tithe at all. The thing being, he clearly narrates to the church in Corinth that Cephas or Apostle Peter is collecting dues, but he of necessity chose not to collect dues from the church in Corinth. Though not collecting from them, he still tells them it is right of the one who serves at the altar of God to be given the dues. Since they have to live by the things of the altar or the gospel. Paul of his own discourse thought it was not fitting to take a tithe of the church at Corinth and yet he took of the churches of the coast of Achaia Yet out of his choice and consent he did collect tithe of all the churches of the realm of Macedonia. That is why he says he is not taking any of the dues of the altar from Corinth: but it does not mean he did not take the dues from other churches. He did and confess still in the second letter to the Corinthians that Macedonia and Achaia are providing for his course and life by taking wages of them; simply put tithe or dues.

2 Corinthians 11:7-12 KJV *Have I committed an offence in abasing myself that ye might be exalted, because I have preached to you the gospel of God freely? I robbed other churches, taking wages of them, to do you service. And when I was present with you, and wanted, I was chargeable to no man: for that which was lacking to me the brethren which came from Macedonia supplied: and in all things I have kept myself from being burdensome unto you, and so will I keep myself. As the truth of Christ is in me, no man shall stop me of this boasting in the regions of Achaia. Wherefore? Because I love you not? God knoweth. But what I do, that I will do, that I may cut off occasion from them which desire occasion; that wherein they glory, they may be found even as we.*

All the time and needed sacrifices to serve are easily attainable when the servant of God can separate fully himself from earth service to the work of God. He is as an enlisted man. Going back to his civil duties eat of the mandate of God and hinders his service. That is why the Macedonians and the inhabitants of Achaia were more culture and fit. There the servant of God could take more time to educate and prepare a fitting bride for the coming of the Lord. The dues unburden God's servants to focus on the ideal of life everlasting and for the perfecting of the saints.

2 Timothy 2:2-7, 10-12 KJV *And the things that thou hast heard of me among many witnesses, the same commit thou to faithful men, who shall be able to teach others also. Thou therefore endure hardness, as a good soldier of Jesus Christ.*

No man that warreth entangleth himself with the affairs of this life; that he may please him who hath chosen him to be a soldier. And if a man also strive for masteries, yet is he not crowned, except he strive lawfully. The husbandman that laboureth must be first partaker of the fruits. Consider what I say; and the Lord give thee understanding in all things. Therefore I endure all things for the elect's sakes, that they may also obtain the salvation which is in Christ Jesus with eternal glory. It is a faithful saying: For if we be dead with him, we shall also live with him: If we suffer, we shall also reign with him: if we deny him, he also will deny us:

The exaltation of Paul to Timothy teaches us something. That he is saying to Timothy that the husband man will partake of the first fruits. The dues being tithe and first fruits are that lot his hope to maintain hold self through the tough walk though a sickly man. He is encouraged to entrust the truth to worthy men, so they may see to his upkeep and he may be able to save a seed for Christ.

Luke 9:57-62 KJV *And it came to pass, that, as they went in the way, a certain man said unto him, Lord, I will follow thee whithersoever thou goest. And Jesus said unto him, Foxes have holes, and birds of the air have nests; but the Son of man hath not where to lay his head. And he said unto another, Follow me. But he said, Lord, suffer me first to go and bury my father. Jesus said unto him, Let the dead bury their dead: but go thou and preach the kingdom of God. And another also said, Lord, I will follow thee; but let me first go bid them farewell, which are at home at my house. And Jesus said unto him, No man, having put his hand to the plough, and looking back, is fit for the kingdom of God.*

The above statement of Christ saying he has no where to lay His head is mostly interpreted as meaning He was lacking; but it mostly borrows from the ideal of the engagement of the work. He weighed abiding places to the course of the overly moving ministry. A thing we soon hear of Paul.

1 Corinthians 4:11 KJV *Even unto this present hour we both hunger, and thirst, and are naked, and are buffeted, and have no certain dwellingplace;*

The account of Christ is mostly aimed at serving and being in one holding place. That is why it is followed by two cases of men who want to be called to go with Him but are regarding their civil duties before the work of Christ. He simply deemed them not fit as He told the first guy He has no abiding structures to be there and be at ease. The course of His purpose was not a life of ease, yet as one would tell though the dedicated church was small it was providing for Him during the cause of His ministry. It is through their dues that He and the twelve were sustained. One can tell of the same course and cause also Paul has no dwellingplace or abiding home.

Luke 8:1-3 KJV *And it came to pass afterward, that he went throughout every city and village, preaching and shewing the glad tidings of the kingdom of God: and the twelve were with him, And certain women, which had been healed of evil spirits and infirmities, Mary called Magdalene, out of whom went seven devils, And Joanna the wife of Chuza Herod's steward, and Susanna, and many others, which ministered unto him of their substance.*

The above words shows you why it always seemed the ministry of Christ was at ease and He did not try to squeeze favor out of the rich or take to the company of the perverse. The altar of service was sufficiently maintained by those of the company whom He had helped. It is more like the confession of Paul that because of the work, he has no abiding home nor is he chargeable to a single abiding place, expressing further the perils and the hardships of the much travel born of the purpose of God. So, obviously in places where the church did not maintain their altars or pay dues he mostly suffered lacked and all. A thing that Christ was saved from by the ideal that the Jews whom He served exclusively among already knew about tithing; that the one who serves the altar of God live by the altar of God. A thing that Paul had to learn the harder way, he was sent to those naive of the way to be schooled of the first things of the principles of God.

2 Corinthians 11:16-30 KJV *I say again, Let no man think me a fool; if otherwise, yet as a fool receive me, that I may boast myself a little. That which I speak, I speak it not after the Lord, but as it were foolishly, in this confidence of boasting. Seeing that many glory after the flesh, I will glory also. For ye suffer fools gladly, seeing ye yourselves are wise. For ye suffer, if a man bring you into bondage, if a man devour you, if a man take of you, if a man exalt himself, if a man smite you on the face. I speak as concerning reproach, as though we had been weak. Howbeit whereinsoever any is bold, (I speak foolishly,) I am bold also. Are they Hebrews? So am I. Are they Israelites? So am I. Are they the seed of Abraham? So am I. Are they ministers of Christ? (I speak as a fool) I am more; in labours more abundant, in stripes above measure, in prisons more frequent, in deaths oft. Of the Jews five times received I forty stripes save one. Thrice was I beaten with rods, once was I stoned, thrice I suffered shipwreck, a night and a day I have been in the deep; In journeyings often, in perils of waters, in perils of robbers, in perils by mine own countrymen, in perils by the heathen, in perils in the city, in perils in the wilderness, in perils in the sea, in perils among false brethren; In weariness and painfulness, in watchings often, in hunger and thirst, in fastings often, in cold and nakedness. Beside those things that are without, that which cometh upon me daily, the care of all the churches. Who is weak, and I am not weak? Who is offended, and I burn not? If I must needs glory, I will glory of the things which concern mine infirmities.*

Below are a list of things that the church is expected to manifest. So, they need a guide and dedicated service men and women who can give themselves to manifesting these abilities in them. The servants of God or the five fold ministry or four fold as called at times are manifested to be the servants of God to guide and teach the church how to relate with God and to grow in to the fullness of Christ. Their due pay or wages will deflect them from being in between as Paul was making and maintaining tents and going to do God's service when free in the coasts of Corinth. Whereas he was more productive in Macedonia and Achaia as those had much time to teach and prepare could even provide his wages when he was working else where.

Ephesians 4:17-32 KJV *This I say therefore, and testify in the Lord, that ye henceforth walk not as other Gentiles walk, in the vanity of their mind, Having the understanding darkened, being alienated from the life of God through the ignorance that is in them, because of the blindness of their heart: Who being past feeling have given themselves over unto lasciviousness, to work all uncleanness with greediness. But ye have not so learned Christ; If so be that ye have heard him, and have been taught by him, as the truth is in Jesus: That ye put off concerning the former conversation the old man, which is corrupt according to the deceitful lusts; And be renewed in the spirit of your mind; And that ye put on the new man, which after God is created in righteousness and true holiness. Wherefore putting away lying, speak every man truth with his neighbour: for we are members one of another. Be ye angry, and sin not: let not the sun go down upon your wrath: Neither give place to the devil. Let him that stole steal no more: but rather let him labour, working with his hands the thing which is good, that he may have to give to him that needeth. Let no corrupt communication proceed out of your mouth, but that which is good to the use of edifying, that it may minister grace unto the hearers. And grieve not the holy Spirit of God, whereby ye are sealed unto the day of redemption. Let all bitterness, and wrath, and anger, and clamour, and evil speaking, be put away from you, with all malice: And be ye kind one to another, tenderhearted, forgiving one another, even as God for Christ's sake hath forgiven you.*

Studying the above words one can easily tell why there are so many chaos and ills happening in the church in Corinth like sicknesses and plagues. Paul could not afford them the time for they were not servicing the altar of God. They could not pay their dues mostly because their mannerism a thing that made Paul exclude them totally from paying dues. He did not want it to seem they are buying him. So it is said of the evils and the sicknesses that did plague that God forsaken gathering.

1 Corinthians 11:26-30 KJV *For as often as ye eat this bread, and drink this cup, ye do shew the Lord's death till he come. Wherefore whosoever shall eat this bread, and drink this cup of the Lord, unworthily, shall be guilty of the body and blood of the Lord. But let a man examine himself, and so let him eat of that bread, and drink of that cup. For he that eateth and drinketh unworthily, eateth and drinketh damnation to himself, not discerning the Lord's body. For this cause many are weak and sickly among you, and many sleep.*

1 Corinthians 5:1-13 KJV *It is reported commonly that there is fornication among you, and such fornication as is not so much as named among the Gentiles, that one should have his father's wife. And ye are puffed up, and have not rather mourned, that he that hath done this deed might be taken away from among you. For I verily, as absent in body, but present in spirit, have judged already, as though I were present, concerning him that hath so done this deed, In the name of our Lord Jesus Christ, when ye are gathered together, and my spirit, with the power of our Lord Jesus Christ, To deliver such an one unto Satan for the destruction of the flesh, that the spirit may be saved in the day of the Lord Jesus. Your glorying is not good.*

Know ye not that a little leaven leaveneth the whole lump? Purge out therefore the old leaven, that ye may be a new lump, as ye are unleavened. For even Christ our passover is sacrificed for us: Therefore let us keep the feast, not with old leaven, neither with the leaven of malice and wickedness; but with the unleavened bread of sincerity and truth. I wrote unto you in an epistle not to company with fornicators: Yet not altogether with the fornicators of this world, or with the covetous, or extortioners, or with idolaters; for then must ye needs go out of the world. But now I have written unto you not to keep company, if any man that is called a brother be a fornicator, or covetous, or an idolater, or a railer, or a drunkard, or an extortioner; with such an one no not to eat. For what have I to do to judge them also that are without? Do not ye judge them that are within? But them that are without God judgeth. Therefore put away from among yourselves that wicked person.

So one last sure word about dues; no dues no plausible service. The servant have to serve at ease in order to deliver. Christ served at ease for there was company of dedicated people giving the providence. Supporting the course of His service with the site dues that they had to give to sustain His calling sure. So, the altar that the servant of God stands upon takes away his or her time and even preparing and continually restoring his virtue to go back and serve there is hard work. So with the dues paid, many more as you were helped would be helped. It was in part, due to the service of that little flock that the Lord was able to be sustained and maintained until the day of the cross; where all humanity was helped. It might seem vague but it is integral that your share should be duly and timeously pitched in. Then when we stand more will be helped. So, they serviced the altar of God not just for themselves but also for others who will need the same help they had.

Luke 8:1-3 KJV *And it came to pass afterward, that he went throughout every city and village, preaching and shewing the glad tidings of the kingdom of God: and the twelve were with him, And certain women, which had been healed of evil spirits and infirmities, Mary called Magdalene, out of whom went seven devils, And Joanna the wife of Chuza Herod's steward, and Susanna, and many others, which ministered unto him of their substance.*

The Conclusive Interpretation Of Tithing

THE CONCLUSIVE ENDING ON DUES

Usually people has a thing to say about their local pastor;

When he/she prays for me I do not get the anticipated results.

When he/she prays for my health I do not heal.

When he/she leads or teaches I cannot hear or understand.

The secret is not in being familiar or getting used to the pastor's teaching. The secret is in another principle being the **Principle Of Agreement**; does the Spirit in him/her recognize you as a member of that congregation or church?

Meaning are you a sheep in that flock?

A thing that is not defined by your regularity but your commitment to being a sheep in that specific kraal of God; paying for the care and hospitality of that house. Burning its lamp by paying the dues, so the church worker can pay their own dues too. A thing that definitely usually your employer deliberately do, so you may pay your dues too. So, in receiving your pay and well in time; you should also as your part do pay your dues to God in time. The thing being; God also has employees to pay and they too ought to be paid in time. Lest you make God a bad character, fellow or chap. Since those people do often entirely trust in Him.

In simple terms: are you paying your tithes?

The tithing issue does not just begin and end with you. It begins with being a portion ascertained God for the service He renders you through human service and those men and women have to take their children to school and buy food and even have a pension to lean on once they retire from Christian service. Unless you are in a mainline church (where they usually just talk about God; and do not show any thing manifest of Him): it takes prayer and a lot of self separation to prepare one for God's service a thing comparable to you taking time to serve in your administrative career or anywhere you serve.

This issue does not just end with the one laying the tithe. It also go to those receiving them; a prevalent thing in the Pentecostal churches is tithe is usually used to buy sound and lighting and other building and construction projects and it should not be so. Especially where the church grows well, the tithe is no longer laid at the feet of the workers of the church but the church board turns it to their own use and disposal which is diabolical.

The tithe was not introduced to God's congregation by the Law or by the purpose of building the church: but it was in produced by the sons of Levi when they turned on each other. It was introduced for the purpose of taking care of them for they separated self to God. So, even in a season where God chooses pastors according to His heart; the tithe is to safe keep and aid the church worker and the pastor maintain their wellbeing and safe guard their retirement.

It is why it was introduced to the congregation of God and it ought to stay so.

The prevalent thing being: if you are not paying your tithe you are not part of the sheep but the society. Your situations would not respond to the voice of the shepherd of that house because you are not a sheep under him. A thing that many young pastors/ prophets often do is cause people to pay a certain fee to be seen. A thing that makes them pay in to the altar so that they may be for that moment be reconciled for the time being. A thing that means as soon as they leave the place their said word of prophecy or healing may be endangered or totally lost. A thing that by principle would mean something worse, not the former disease will plague the incumbent of such a service. They simply sell temporal aid to the destruction of those who buy it.

Luke 11:21-26 KJV *When a strong man armed keepeth his palace, his goods are in peace: But when a stronger than he shall come upon him, and overcome him, he taketh from him all his armour wherein he trusted, and divideth his spoils. He that is not with me is against me: and he that gathereth not with me scattereth. When the unclean spirit is gone out of a man, he walketh through dry places, seeking rest; and finding none, he saith, I will return unto my house whence I came out. And when he cometh, he findeth it swept and garnished. Then goeth he, and taketh to him seven other spirits more wicked than himself; and they enter in, and dwell there: and the last state of that man is worse than the first.*

THE APOSTLES' FAULTS: IN THE DUES

Acts 4:34-37 KJV *Neither was there any among them that lacked: for as many as were possessors of lands or houses sold them, and brought the prices of the things that were sold, And laid them down at the apostles' feet: and distribution was made unto every man according as he had need. And Joses, who by the apostles was surnamed Barnabas, (which is, being interpreted, The son of consolation,) a Levite, and of the country of Cyprus, Having land, sold it, and brought the money, and laid it at the apostles' feet.*

Many people when it comes to the early church are taken by the expression; an they lacked nothing. Simplistically the apostles did condone the ideal of the brethren selling everything they have and laying it at the feet of the apostles. A thing that soon gave a tremendous lack to the church in Jerusalem as they did have to depend on Paul and Barnabas' collection from other churches. For a new term was soon heard; the poor among them. Many soon argue why did not the church continue as it did from the beginning?

The truth is. The actual first church which was mostly converted Jews as it began in Jerusalem was soon plagued by lack. Not because God was not among them, but rather because the apostles did not contain the excitement of the people. It does not just show in the dismantling of the dues ethic but also the Baptism instruction of Christ. They were clearly told to baptize in the name of the Father, the Son and the Holy Spirit; but they never did that even once. Because of the excitement, they did only baptize in the name of Jesus Christ; a deliberate disobedience of what Christ explicitly said.

So, excitement always makes people ask. The above question but never set them on the ideal that the same church was soon plagued by poverty. The same story also is often missed by the life of King Solomon. People are always excited by the ideal that he began his reign a rich man but none looks at the reason why his son had to depend on charging or exhorting tribute from his own people. It means his father died a terribly poor man if the first thing he has to be asked to reduce is tribute exhorted from Israel. It means the man had to no capacity to service a thousand women. A thing contrary to the law of God that was the ordained measure of the time.

Deuteronomy 17:14-20 KJV *When thou art come unto the land which the LORD thy God giveth thee, and shalt possess it, and shalt dwell therein, and shalt say, I will set a king over me, like as all the nations that are about me; Thou shalt in any wise set him king over thee, whom the LORD thy God shall choose: one from among thy brethren shalt thou set king over thee: thou mayest not set a stranger over thee, which is not thy brother. But he shall not multiply horses to himself, nor cause the people to return to Egypt, to the end that he should multiply horses: forasmuch as the LORD hath said unto you, Ye shall henceforth return no more that way. Neither shall he multiply wives to himself, that his heart turn not away: neither shall he greatly multiply to himself silver and gold. And it shall be, when he sitteth upon the throne of his kingdom, that he shall write him a copy of this law in a book out of that which is before the priests the Levites: And it shall be with him, and he shall read therein all the days of his life: that he may learn to fear the LORD his God, to keep all the words of this law and these statutes, to do them: That his heart be not lifted up above his brethren, and that he turn not aside from the commandment, to the right hand, or to the left: to the end that he may prolong his days in his kingdom, he, and his children, in the midst of Israel.*

In the skeptics of oversight we often miss the truth by simply thinking it ended as it began. Without pondering carefully to see the end of each and every matter; which is the reason why the past of these men and women are shared with us, so that we may do otherwise. That is why we often miss things like the writings above; God had never condoned polygamy but it seemed a norm of the time. Not by His desire but by the deviation of the subjects as even the first king being Saul was a polygamous man. It is also key and of uttermost importance to learn that Christ never said to the apostles that they should tell people to go and sell their all and bring to the church. Meaning, they should have cautioned and enquired when it happened. Yet they kept silent until there were the needy among them and they no longer had things among them all. Paul had to burden the work of constantly gathering offerings from the gentile churches for the church in Jerusalem. A thing he had to make look like it had somehow hidden blessings in it though born of the apostles' faults.

A thing that meant the communal living that was availed by the sudden plenty of selling their all when it subsided there were issues. Issues including lack.

THE KINGDOM OF GOD HERE ON EARTH.

The kingdom of God here on earth as of now is like any other corporation or government existent here on earth. It has costs and overheads like any running corporation. Man hours are spent of dedicated singles and family men. They all need to be compensated for those man hours or their lives and bills will be unpaid; yet they being spent.

In simple essence like any who receives a service here on earth; for God's service you must be ready to pay as for any other service. So, the dues as a levy due for their paid or given reason. In simple terms, if you opt out of giving; do also opt out of attending a physical church. It is someone's offering that did build the structure you lifted your hands and gave your life to Christ in. So, if you are kingdom minded; as someone provided for them tent or place you got baptized in, you should pass on the due recompense for the kingdom to expand and reach others. Any that does not tithe or give offering by choice is not by any means answerable to God nor is God answerable to him/her. The simple thing being by principle God works through men and those abiding structures that are being funded by the dues.

The ideal being, if you are not responsible for the physical build and running of the kingdom, you are like one absconding or dodging to pay tax in a country and are an alien in the kingdom of God. To use the things and personnel of the kingdom of God you have to maintain and service the wares and beings who serve the kingdom. It is the simplistic and conclusive interpretation of dues. If they be relevant, then the personnel and the church buildings must be relevant and vice verse. The gospel needs personnel and structure to function well as an organized kingdom. That is why it exacts a set due or pay from those who live by it as those who live in a set nation. Without the dues the personnel evade their tasks and without the personnel there is no progress or progression.

That is the principle of seedtime and harvest in full.
It does not begin with us and will not end with us. It is the key principle that began with humanity occupying earth. It does not begin with Abraham or Jacob but it goes all the way back to the sure beginning. We often say the first person to pay tithe is Abraham. In part it is true, but one would say Abraham is the first person to voluntarily pay tithe. As for Adam and Eve it was mandatory; they were only given fruit and herbs with seed inside to eat. So they may saw back in

to the soil to expand the field for the expansion of humanity. The more the people; the more the seed needed to serve and maintain them.

Genesis 1:29 KJV *And God said, Behold, I have given you every herb bearing seed, which is upon the face of all the earth, and every tree, in the which is the fruit of a tree yielding seed; to you it shall be for meat.*

It is deliberate that God gives man and his wife only the things that bear seed. In simple terms God is saying, in every fruit I give you or herb to eat; there is seed to saw back in to the ground. So you may not just care for but expand the garden so that you and your kids may be full. Or else the fruits will always be enough for you and your wife only. So, seedtime and harvest or the principle of dues is not just meant for you. It was created to take care of things that matter to you. All the physical things that belong to you are taken care of by the tithe one way or the other. The ideal being; if the first lump be holy. Then the rest of your things are untouchable to the enemy; they are holy. Because in paying your tithe you are securing them from the chief thief who is the influencer of all the minor thieves; the devil.

In simple terms, tithe like tax give your state the right to protect and serve you and your property and family; tithe gives the kingdom of God the right to defend what belongs to you by rite. It says even though they are not born of God, all they have and use is declared holy by your paid dues. Until and unless they are no longer under your care; which means by then they should have a measure of security of their own by their own salvation. Mentioning salvation, it does defend and offer you the rite to be a member of the coming earth. Yet until we are apprehended we are under the care of human shepherds who they and their house hold depend on God through the tax or levy that you must pay to be maintained by God through them.

Adam and Eve were told to replenish the earth from standing in a garden. A thing that meant they had to do something for the garden to be the supply of the whole earth. It meant for the sake of the increase they were supposed to enterprise, so the supply may be continuous and fitting for the growth and expansion in numbers. The seed was a form of defense and security for the task they were blessed with to fulfill. As long as they had the supply of food they tended for; from within the supply there was always seed to expand and provide even the more for humanity. That is the simplistic interpretation of the purpose of tithe to this time. For more humanity to come in and to be accommodated according to the pattern of God; more and more tithe must be supplied for the more and more work to be accomplished through well paid men.

The workman is worthy of his meat as the Lord Jesus did say.

Matthew 10:5-10 KJV *These twelve Jesus sent forth, and commanded them, saying, Go not into the way of the Gentiles, and into any city of the Samaritans enter ye not: But go rather to the lost sheep of the house of Israel. And as ye go, preach, saying, The kingdom of heaven is at hand. Heal the sick, cleanse the lepers, raise the dead, cast out devils: freely ye have* *received, freely give. Provide neither gold, nor silver, nor brass in your purses, Nor scrip for your journey, neither two coats, neither shoes, nor yet staves: for the workman is worthy of his meat.*

He did send the apostles when they had no abiding structures or stock of beings to take care of. They literally just needed what to eat for the sum of their souls and that is what Christ asked them to ask for; just food to replenish their needs. It was also so with the Lord that He had no cause to demand much from the church so it just took care of his daily needs.

Luke 8:1-3 KJV *And it came to pass afterward, that he went throughout every city and village, preaching and shewing the glad tidings of the kingdom of God: and the twelve were with him, And certain women, which had been healed of evil spirits and infirmities, Mary called Magdalene, out of whom went seven devils, And Joanna the wife of Chuza Herod's steward, and Susanna, and many others, which ministered unto him of their substance.*

This to sum the concept of dues. The Holy Bible says there were not just some women but many others who took care of Christ's work out of their substance. A thing that meant He did not preach the gospel out of His expenditure but of the church that He had raised. They did take care of the work; so it may reach others. Mind you; the Holy Bible does not say they controlled Him by their substance but says they provided for Him meaning His work and livelihood; as means him and the apostles and the work.

It is mandatory that whosoever serves the gospel; as Christ was provided for by the gospel should live by the gospel. As did Christ so did the apostles. Even the apostle of the gentiles did take wages of the church to sup up his needs. It is the beneficiation of giving self a gift to the church and the course of the greater good. It should not be a place of suffering and confusion but a sure and clear providence by God through His church to His servants.

It is as Christ says; if you are being taxed to be under Caesar's domain pay his levies and if you are under God's domain also be sure to pay His dues.

Mark 12:13-17 KJV *And they send unto him certain of the Pharisees and of the Herodians, to catch him in his words. And when they were come, they say unto him, Master, we know that thou art true, and carest for no man: for thou regardest not the person of men, but teachest the way of God in truth: Is it lawful to give tribute to Caesar, or not? Shall we give, or shall we not give? But he, knowing their hypocrisy, said unto them, Why tempt ye me? Bring me a penny, that I may see it. And they brought it. And he saith unto them, Whose is this image and superscription? And they said unto him, Caesar's. And Jesus answering said unto them, Render to Caesar the things that are Caesar's, and to God the things that are God's. And they marvelled at him.*

One thing that is usually misconstrued about the above words of Christ is that He actually talked about two levies that are paid in to two kingdoms. The kingdom of God and the kingdom that belonged to Rome at that time. He said pay the due levies to Caesar and also pay the due levies to God. It is not about the physical and the Spiritual but both about the physical things that are dues in both rules.

Tithe of Tithes

The Setman

The Setman.

Where is the Setman in the modern church?

During the pilgrimage from Egypt to Canaan arose men of the company of Levi. Men that God had called close to do the service of the temple did rise against the priesthood of Aaron and say we are holy and fit to do everything as Moses and Aaron. One would point out one thing; the Holy Bible says they were princes of the assembly, choice men of renown and were famous men among the congregation. That is they were men of influence among the people.

They rose to rebel against the Setman being Aaron. They obviously would not approach the seat of Moses the Judge but we're obviously weighing Aaron's worth for he as them spoke through Moses. A thing that causes Moses to soon detect and rise to the occasion. He could see it was not against him but his brother and his Setman Aaron (for Moses was unto him as God) and he was Setman instead of Moses by Moses' choice.

Exodus 4:16 KJV *And he shall be thy spokesman unto the people: and he shall be, even he shall be to thee instead of a mouth, and thou shalt be to him instead of God.*

So, it was Aaron's authority that was being challenged and God did revolt and do a new thing before the congregation. If there be a Setman in our season where is that God who guards him jealously? Not just the noise of the church but the government and all's voices have swallowed the Setman in the process. Now the church is led as the government chooses and the Setman is handled as the church board ordains. A thing that makes one to desire the more to know about God's jealousy in the issue.

Is it the issue of the church and government or the church is somehow misinformed to take their stand for the Setman and his God?

Still above it all; Where is God's jealousy one would ask?

The God of old who spoke for Aaron, does he still have a determined lot for the Setman ahead of his congregation or not?

The Holy Bible does not say Moses had to purloin for the humiliating of Aaron the servant of God. It says he fell on his face. He did not go on strike or try to prove his forcefulness but did fall on his face before those who undermine his authority and his brother. He did show God it is a thing instead of him that He should take charge of self. He gave God the audacity to rise by humbling self.

Numbers 16:4-14 KJV *And when Moses heard it, he fell upon his face: And he spake unto Korah and unto all his company, saying, Even to morrow the LORD will shew who are his, and who is holy; and will cause him to come near unto him: even him whom he hath chosen will he cause to come near unto him. This do; Take you censers, Korah, and all his company; And put fire therein, and put incense in them before the LORD to morrow: and it shall be that the man whom the LORD doth choose, he shall be holy: ye take too much upon you, ye sons of Levi. And Moses said unto Korah, Hear, I pray you, ye sons of Levi: Seemeth it but a small thing unto you, that the God of Israel hath separated you from the congregation of Israel, to bring you near to himself to do the service of the tabernacle of the LORD, and to stand before the congregation to minister unto them? And he hath brought thee near to him, and all thy brethren the sons of Levi with thee: and seek ye the priesthood also? For which cause both thou and all thy company are gathered together against the LORD: and what is Aaron, that ye murmur against him? And Moses sent to call Dathan and Abiram, the sons of Eliab: which said, We will not come up: Is it a small thing that thou hast brought us up out of a land that floweth with milk and honey, to kill us in the wilderness, except thou make thyself altogether a prince over us? Moreover thou hast not brought us into a land that floweth with milk and honey, or given us inheritance of fields and vineyards: wilt thou put out the eyes of these men? We will not come up.*

One thing one would soon sense and smell is; they preferred slavery over any form of free enterprising. So, they clearly said they were living in a land of milk and honey as slaves to the Egyptians who beat and killed them at will. It was a brewing rebellion against the mandate of God.

So, even the new Setman is like is constantly faced with challenge and resistance and has to constantly prove self. Constantly calling self anointed. Constantly telling people he has their things in him. Constantly telling people it is through his anointing and grace that they are healed and delivered.

One would say the much labor is to prove self rather than to lead God's people. Though understanding all the above that is constantly said is not in part or otherwise true. Just lures to pull the followership by a means of cunning strings. A thing that means most would die not knowing the truth.

In the name of putting a morsel upon the table to sustain his own house. Many are lost. A thing that makes one question the genuineness of the call now our days if all have to be parading to keep the church keen and forth coming in communication in giving and receiving. A thing that causes one to question;

Where is God in the midst of the noise of this generation?

The office in the midst of the noise is taken by too much empty talk. A thing that makes one question the modern Setman's authority. For the Holy Bible says as soon as Moses concluded speaking; God did show up?

Numbers 16:31-35 KJV *And it came to pass, as he had made an end of speaking all these words, that the ground clave asunder that was under them: And the earth opened her mouth, and swallowed them up, and their houses, and all the men that appertained unto Korah, and all their goods. They, and all that appertained to them, went down alive into the pit, and the earth closed upon them: and they perished from among the congregation. And all Israel that were round about them fled at the cry of them: for they said, Lest the earth swallow us up also. And there came out a fire from the LORD, and consumed the two hundred and fifty men that offered incense.*

The fact of the matter remains. Even now the servant of God faces ridicule and much purloining. From men sent even as did the sons of Levi and of the masses and even men not born of God. Yet the profound question still stands.

Can God or would God just stand for him to prove otherwise?

Or he has to continue being the empty gong making much ado noise about self?

In simple terms to fully clarify the cause of the question. Is the Setman still relevant and his office?

A thing that means if there is still a need for a man to stand ahead of the church of God. Then there should be an elaborate hire for his services and for his office. Meaning in dissolving his role's hire you are not just dissolving his hire but the relevance of his call. A thing that caused **Numbers 16** to be written down. Which we shall let most of it show below now.

Numbers 16:1-35 KJV *Now Korah, the son of Izhar, the son of Kohath, the son of Levi, and Dathan and Abiram, the sons of Eliab, and On, the son of Peleth, sons of Reuben, took men: And they rose up before Moses, with certain of the children of Israel, two hundred and fifty princes of the assembly, famous in the congregation, men of renown: And they gathered themselves together against Moses and against Aaron, and said unto them, Ye take too much upon you, seeing all* *the congregation are holy, every one of them, and the LORD is among them: wherefore then lift ye up yourselves above the congregation of the LORD? And when Moses heard it, he fell upon his face: And he spake unto Korah and unto all his company, saying, Even to morrow the LORD will shew who are his, and who is holy; and will cause him to come near unto him: even him whom he hath chosen will he cause to come near unto him. This do; Take you censers, Korah, and all his company; And put fire therein, and put incense in them before the LORD to morrow: and it shall be that the man whom the LORD doth choose, he shall be holy: ye take too much upon you, ye sons of Levi. And Moses said unto Korah, Hear, I pray you, ye sons of Levi: Seemeth it but a small thing unto you, that the God of Israel hath separated you from the congregation of Israel, to bring you near to himself to do the service of the tabernacle of the LORD, and to stand before the congregation to minister unto them? And he hath brought thee near to him, and all thy brethren the sons of Levi with thee: and seek ye the priesthood also? For which cause both thou and all thy company are gathered together against the LORD: and what is Aaron, that ye murmur against him? And Moses sent to call Dathan and Abiram, the sons of Eliab: which said, We will not come up: Is it a small thing that thou hast brought us up out of a land that floweth with milk and honey, to kill us in the wilderness, except thou make thyself altogether a prince over us? Moreover thou hast not brought us into a land that floweth with milk and honey, or given us inheritance of fields and vineyards: wilt thou put out the eyes of these men? We will not come up. And Moses was very wroth, and said unto the LORD, Respect not thou their offering: I have not taken one ass from them, neither have I hurt one of them. And Moses said unto Korah, Be thou and all thy company before the LORD, thou, and they, and Aaron, to morrow:bAnd take every man his censer, and put incense in them, and bring ye before the LORD every man his censer, two hundred and fifty censers; thou also, and Aaron, each of you his censer. And they took every man his censer, and put fire in them, and laid incense thereon, and stood in the door of the tabernacle of the congregation with Moses and Aaron. And Korah gathered all the congregation against them unto the door of the tabernacle of the congregation: and the glory of the LORD appeared unto all the congregation. And the LORD spake unto Moses and unto Aaron, saying, Separate yourselves from among this congregation, that I may consume them in a moment. And they fell upon their faces, and said, O God, the God of the spirits of all flesh, shall one man sin, and wilt thou be wroth with all the congregation? And the LORD spake unto Moses, saying, Speak unto the congregation, saying, Get you up from about the tabernacle of Korah, Dathan, and Abiram. And Moses rose up and went unto Dathan and Abiram; and the elders of Israel followed him. And he spake unto the congregation, saying, Depart, I pray you, from the tents of these wicked men, and touch nothing of their's, lest ye be consumed in all their sins. So they gat up from the tabernacle of Korah, Dathan, and Abiram, on every side: and Dathan and Abiram came out, and stood in the door of their tents, and their wives, and their sons, and their little children. And Moses said, Hereby ye shall know that the LORD hath sent me to do all these works; for I have not done them of mine own mind. If these men die the common death of all men, or if they be visited after the visitation of all men; then the LORD hath not sent me. But if the LORD make a new thing, and the earth open her mouth, and swallow them up, with all that appertain unto them, and they go down quick into the pit; then ye shall understand that these men have provoked the LORD. And it came to pass, as he had made an end of speaking all these words, that the ground clave asunder that was under them: And the earth opened her mouth, and swallowed them up, and their houses, and all the men that appertained unto Korah, and all their goods. They, and all that appertained to them, went down alive into the pit, and the earth closed upon them: and they perished from among the congregation. And all Israel that were round about them fled at the cry of them: for they said, Lest the earth swallow us up also. And there came out a fire from the LORD, and consumed the two hundred and fifty men that offered incense.*

One would not just be mindful of the repercussive instant renditions of God only on the case of the rebellion of Israel and even the voices of His judges through the ages. As with Joshua and even with Samson and Deborah and the other judges like Samuel. What happened to the ordained strength of the Setman in the congregation's disasters and all. They had an impactful audacity to even stop the cause of the sun to do God's service in their days.

Joshua 10:11-14 KJV *And it came to pass, as they fled from before Israel, and were in the going down to Beth-horon, that the LORD cast down great stones from heaven upon them unto Azekah, and they died: they were more which died with hailstones than they whom the children of Israel slew with the sword. Then spake Joshua to the LORD in the day when the LORD delivered up the Amorites before the children of Israel, and he said in the sight of Israel, Sun, stand thou still upon Gibeon; and thou, Moon, in the valley of Ajalon. And the sun stood still, and the moon stayed, until the people had avenged themselves upon their enemies. Is not this written in the book of Jasher? So the sun stood still in the midst of heaven, and hasted not to go down about a whole day. And there was no day like that before it or after it, that the LORD hearkened unto the voice of a man: for the LORD fought for Israel.*

Does this have to do with us abandoning his lot?

Or the man that is born and ordained to stand ahead of God's children has lost both relevance and place?

Is it now safe even right to say the Setman is nowhere in the modern church?

In simple terms the Setman has no elaborate hire nor sure standard of both his pay or rite of worth or value. Rather he is treated to the worth acclaimed or soon self proclaimed by him before the church. The question is;

Is God still in the business of sending men with an independent vision and mission?

How is He held accountable for the man hours they serve?
    And also;

Who is held accountable for his care; being the Setman?
   In simple terms;

What is the lot or the portion of the Setman in the church?

Does he or does he not have a sure way to remunerate?

Not by trial and error or anyhow the church chooses to value or weigh his hire.

Did God set a standard?

Or; Does any have the capacity to decide anyhow how he is remunerated or how is he kept as the gift of the church?

Did God give a sure outline about his upkeep and maintenance?

Or only during the sundry times any can decide the fate of the Setman by deciding whether he is the gift duly given and cared for by the church?

It takes ought to heed and listen. Since the Setman is the same man who God gave the vision and mandate used to start the said church and soon it is found out that it has to be the mandate of the man to see it come to pass or die in its flowers. Yet in the likelihood that it picks off, constitutionally it is not fine or right for him to stand at its head. A thing that means in the struggle and setting up of the church, the Setman yeans all the things that have to start it up; but once it takes root he has to watch from a distance.

Then when it happens; who has the spiritual rite to watch out for him; For he has been entrusted with a mission and a vision to go ahead of the church of God?

As means church is his all pertaining to livelihood and man hours spent laboring in prayer and fastings and preparation way before he is made ready to serve. It took Moses forty years of preparation though he passed on the stick to be shared by him and his brother. He did have to labor in preparation in a priest's house in the desert: forty solid years. Yet what Korah and his company could see was the maneuvering mandate and the now things before them.

A thing that men often miss is that there is a stage called preparation where the Setman has to be made ready. A thing that both costs resources and life in man hours. Elijah was told to go in to hiding. Moses was forced into exile. Even in the line of kings one would soon mention; David had to serve under the constant peril of King Saul to see how a king is served and leads and manages his affairs. All that men see is David the King; the guy who killed the lion and the bear and they do not count the amount of preparation he had to go through in order to be trusted with the kingship or the leading of the house of God. It is when Moses turns to see and speak to the voice in the fire that men begins to be aware of his call. But it was the forty years running and hiding from Pharaoh that taught him how to trust in God. The forty years of the peril of the desert from the palace that made him Moses; not the Law or the Levitical priesthood.

The patience and the peril of just trusting without resources or a worthy name. A thing that soon makes Moses to question God; who am I and who shall I say has sent me. A thing that did not prove enough until God spoke by living signs.

Exodus 3:11-18 KJV *And Moses said unto God, Who am I, that I should go unto Pharaoh, and that I should bring forth the children of Israel out of Egypt? And he said, Certainly I will be with thee; and this shall be a token unto thee, that I have sent thee: When thou hast brought forth the people out of Egypt, ye shall serve God upon this mountain. And Moses said unto God, Behold, when I come unto the children of Israel, and shall say unto them, The God of your fathers hath sent me unto you; and they shall say to me, What is his name? what shall I say unto them? And God said unto Moses, I AM THAT I AM: and he said, Thus shalt thou say unto the children of Israel, I AM hath sent me unto you. And God said moreover unto Moses, Thus shalt thou say unto the children of Israel, The LORD God of your fathers, the God of Abraham, the God of Isaac, and the God of Jacob, hath sent me unto you: this is my name for ever, and this is my memorial unto all generations. Go, and gather the elders of Israel together, and say unto them, The LORD God of your fathers, the God of Abraham, of Isaac, and of Jacob, appeared unto me, saying, I have surely visited you, and seen that which is done to you in Egypt: And I have said, I will bring you up out of the affliction of Egypt unto the land of the Canaanites, and the Hittites, and the Amorites, and the Perizzites, and the Hivites, and the Jebusites, unto a land flowing with milk and honey. And they shall hearken to thy voice: and thou shalt come, thou and the elders of Israel, unto the king of Egypt, and ye shall say unto him, The LORD God of the Hebrews hath met with us: and now let us go, we beseech thee, three days' journey into the wilderness, that we may sacrifice to the LORD our God.*

It is mostly these trying hours when you just have to trust a voice without any resources or any personnel that one has to endure and prepare even the more. Yet endure the forced changes in to one's life and even the peril of one's life as God did even purpose to kill Moses for the circumcision of his son with the Ethiopian.

Exodus 4:24-26 KJV *And it came to pass by the way in the inn, that the LORD met him, and sought to kill him. Then Zipporah took a sharp stone, and cut off the foreskin of her son, and cast it at his feet, and said, Surely a bloody husband art thou to me. So he let him go: then she said, A bloody husband thou art, because of the circumcision.*

The perils of the travels and the cost of hoisting the family about.

Yet in all these things one would ask; does he have a hire to reimburse not just for his hire now? To look in to the endured servitude and the years of getting God's message. Not just to preach but also to relate by his meekness exemplary leadership.

This does not just end with the church but also the political authorities for they have reduced the Setman to be an underling in the church coming after the whole church committee. In essence legally the Setman does not stand as the head of the church even though he is the carrier and originator of the vision and the mission of the church. The thing that means there is a team put before them by the authority of the earth to rule and govern over the Setman. Meaning the Setman is not set to be the last voice of the church but a contributing factor; a thing that makes them but a voice among the many. Not an eloquent lead as a voice sent to direct the church of God.

The simple question is; what are the dues of the church towards their own Setman?

The Setman in any modern church setting is one person who many do not know how to take care of. In general people start trying to raise seed for him even go beyond the necessary thinking pleasing him would place them in place to win the favor of God.

What naturally places us in the favor of God is knowing Him and following Him. Christ says I am the door and whosoever enters by Me will find pasture. Meaning our providence is not in the servant of God but in Christ; who if you really do enter in by Him you are naturally well provided for.

Surprisingly the word does not say so. It says if you do a thing for a man because of their class or height; you will gain the gift of that height. Which means it is not the gift from God but what is in the personal ability of the man. A thing that means one has to be careful where they are aimed to receive from; whether from God or a man, sent or not.

Matthew 10:40-42 KJV *He that receiveth you receiveth me, and he that receiveth me receiveth him that sent me. He that receiveth a prophet in the name of a prophet shall receive a prophet's reward; and he that receiveth a righteous man in* *the name of a righteous man shall receive a righteous man's reward. And whosoever shall give to drink unto one of these little ones a cup of cold water only in the name of a disciple, verily I say unto you, he shall in no wise lose his reward.*

Matthew 18:5 KJV *And whoso shall receive one such little child in my name receiveth me.*

Luke 14:12-14 KJV *Then said he also to him that bade him, When thou makest a dinner or a supper, call not thy friends, nor thy brethren, neither thy kinsmen, nor thy rich neighbours; lest they also bid thee again, and a recompence be made thee. But when thou makest a feast, call the poor, the maimed, the lame, the blind: And thou shalt be blessed; for they cannot recompense thee: for thou shalt be recompensed at the resurrection of the just.*

A thing that instead rather brings more bees than butterflies.

In simple terms it all adds up to having an income. It is those who have an income that seem to be taking care of the servant of God; whether good or not. Whether saved or not. It is more of the beneficiation rather than being provided for in a godly way. A thing that would often mean the same well-off people are the inner circle of the servant of God whether newbies or seasoned; mature or naïve. The inconsistency often found in the church of God regarding revenue is the one that usually cause the servant of God to be deliberately liaised with a certain group of people or family in regard with communication in giving and receiving.

The problem of the failing dues.

So, in the event of the servant of God being in such a situation that is often than not. Such families literally run the church and are placed ahead of it. A thing that would mean testimonies about monies and things instead of the way of God. They start calling the proud happy and blessed. They truncate the blessedness of God for the pride of life and the earthly substance the measure of the blessedness in God; a false balance as far as the truth goes.

Luke 12:13-21 KJV *And one of the company said unto him, Master, speak to my brother, that he divide the inheritance with me. And he said unto him, Man, who made me a judge or a divider over you? And he said unto them, Take heed, and beware of covetousness: for a man's life consisteth not in the abundance of the things which he possesseth. And he spake a parable unto them, saying, The ground of a certain rich man brought forth plentifully: And he thought within himself, saying, What shall I do, because I have no room where to bestow my fruits? And he said, This will I do: I will pull down my barns, and build greater; and there will I bestow all my fruits and my goods. And I will say to my soul, Soul, thou hast much goods laid up for many years; take thine ease, eat, drink, and be merry. But God said unto him, Thou fool, this night thy* *soul shall be required of thee: then whose shall those things be, which thou hast provided? So is he that layeth up treasure for himself, and is not rich toward God.*

Though Christ clearly said the life of a man does not consist of the abundance of things he possesses; the new church seems to agree otherwise. It is a constant parade of earthly things that is being used as a measure of being blessed or not. An obvious heretic exploitation of the truth. A thing that even the saints of old were warned against.

Malachi 3:14-18 KJV *Ye have said, It is vain to serve God: and what profit is it that we have kept his ordinance, and that we have walked mournfully before the LORD of hosts? And now we call the proud happy; yea, they that work wickedness are set up; yea, they that tempt God are even delivered. Then they that feared the LORD spake often one to another: and the LORD hearkened, and heard it, and a book of remembrance was written before him for them that feared the LORD, and that thought upon his name. And they shall be mine, saith the LORD of hosts, in that day when I make up my jewels; and I will spare them, as a man spareth his own son that serveth him. Then shall ye return, and discern between the righteous and the wicked, between him that serveth God and him that serveth him not.*

This is the beginning of any given church; a man with a sure message carrying a vision and mission that says what has to be done and what kind of church has to be started. It all begins with that. Then the word that breaks of the intents and direction that has to be taken and set up starts way before church boards and public meetings. It all starts under the roof or place of a single sent man of a set home stead and then it can spread further on.

And that is the task and the beginning of a Setman.

As he picks a place and a people to lead it is all about fulfilment but the most of the job is getting the vision, mission and the message that he has for the people from God. And that is what keeps and maintains his purpose; the objectives of what he has been sent to do. And to do those he needs the enablers and other parts that makes a vision speak. The reflecting and sounding boards in men set to lift the vision and mission granted him as of necessity of God's providence by merit born of servitude not placement in society or hierarchy of materials. Not a name or substance but the due savor of God in the should be the key mandate and that completes the work of God through that is set before God's people to fulfill a set purpose for a set season.

Then when it is all done one has to ask;

What is his hire?

Tithe

Tithe?

The wise may shake the head and pretend to know but the word tithe is one little peculiar one. Whether High Tithe or Common Tithe or Festival Tithe one would first like to know the origination of the name tithe. Unlike much of the word it is real surprising that though the word tithe is the most domineering when it comes to paying the dues; it is an English secular word. It is not born of any old Hebrew like other Old Testament words neither of Latin or Greek as most New Testament words.

The word tithe is born of old ordinal numeral in English, that goes back to a prehistoric West Germanic spelling; **Tehuntha**. One should observe carefully to understand that it is formed from the cardinal numeral **Tehun** simply meaning **Ten**, thus being brought to a fraction that is a tenth becoming **Teogothian**. **Teogothian** simply means that, a **Tenth** in Old English, and the same ordinal suffix that has survived in to Modern English as; **-th** shedding **Ian** in the process of time.

Moving from its numeric emphasis the grammatical and etymon carries us to the current word Tithe. One should know the travel of the word tenth had not just taken many forms before it became tithe. Among the British it has revolved to a former that only differs not by the silent latter but one letter being; Y causing it to only differ in writing as **Tythe**. The grammatical narrative translates thus; Tithe is from the Middle English nominal noun **Tighethe** (**Ti(ghe)the**). The fiddles are born of that original word in Old English being **Teogotha** which actually means tenth but one here should understand that also its active or actual action of taking the said part is **Teogothian** also simply meaning tenth; as the active noun of taking the tenth.

The Middle English nominal noun **Tighethe** (**Ti(ghe)the**) is where the tide turns and it sincerely adopted the much silence of the last letter; A and began to have a silent center. The middle English did loose the letter; N somewhere within itself from the variant in the verb **Tighten** and the noun **Tighethe**. Though it might be contrary as it might be surprising: this middle English annunciation one would say was deemed to have a purely silent center by the standard of then. It essentially highly influenced the end common word as announcing the two by today's standard matches well. , Old English **Teogotha** tenth; (verb) Middle English **Tithen**, The Old English word of the action to take or exact tithe is **Teogothian** (which makes it an Old English), which is a derivative of the noun; nominal

This is to sum up the etymon and grammatical; though the origination of the end word began with a West Germanic number ten in **Tehun**. The much fiddles and regeneration to the effect of it currently being simply call a tithe happened in the English realm. So, one can safely say it is born of the Old English noun **Teogotha**. The word **Tithe** comes from the Old English **Teothe** or **Teotha** which is a contraction of **Teogotha** meaning a tenth. Meaning it took a change in annunciation by use or by being accommodated as an accepted part of use or familiarity.

One for a discourse could also argue that the middle English version of the noun and verb did do the silencing and the shaping of the word rather than the shortening. For in the middle ages it was announced Tithe; and **Tighethe** that on its own did take away the vowels O and A that was rather massively repercussive on the annunciation then. One would say it is owed to a change in style or trend of the language then. Even then, **Ti(Ghe)The** and **Teotha** notably agree as one would say there was much ado about the classes then. In the engagement of the debutants and the high teas; there were annunciations solely meant to be lady like and gentleman like. Yet there were rough street addresses of the same. May be the lower class opting for the old annunciation **Teothe** and the trendy high class opting for the new sounding **Teotha**. None the less both became desolate to move for **Tythe**, that has also been moved by the refined writing Tithe, though it does not reflect much change on meaning.

All in all, one would say without much further ado that the word Tithe did not travel its scape or broadness from English but a word born of the carry over of the practice from Judaism to Christianity. Though the practice old, the word Tithe was brought in by the inebriation of the English on to the faith. Meaning, the actual original word is not as widespread; as means the original word as from Judaism. A thing that often escapes the naïve being that **Tithe** was not born (does not originate) from Judaism and even the Mosaic or the Old Testament. It might come as a shock or an overwhelming surprise that 430 years before the inception of the Abraham actually did pay a tithe to Melchisedek. A thing that means Judaism incorporated the use of tithe in the congregational system by adoption not by starting it. Meaning the Old Testament and Judaism did find the tithe existent and did systemize it in to Judaism. Where it was refined and institutionalized and the compulsory exacting was passed on to the new church from the early and the church of old. Tithing was passed on through the **Chronicles Of Order** in to Christianity as the **Principle Of Seedtime And Harvest** or the **Dues Ethic**.

So, as light as it may sound. Still it is important to mention that tithe is not an Old Testament Law; but the law found it in place as both Abraham and Jacob did partake of it way before there was even the nation Israel. A thing that means Israel and the Law found it continuing and left it continuing. It was not their invention or the invention of the law or Moses. They joined in and left it as it was; going on.

Then one would say going back to where Judaism found it and began to implement it.

Which Hebrew word was actually translated in to **Teogotha**?

As means the actual word as of the practice as it was done in Judaism.

The Hebrew word **ma'aser** (מעשר) was translated in to the word **Teogotha** being a masculine noun that means "a tenth part".

Tithing was a mandatory practice in ancient Israel; which is a gentle way to say it was an enforced payment or levy of giving a tenth of one's income or property to support the Highpriest, the Levites and the poor. The adoptive mandate of the same did spill in to the church of God. A thing that meant the church as Israel was would be able to be self sufficient in all its endeavors.

The tithe was based on agricultural harvests and the kraal because ancient Israel was an agrarian society. The tithe has three significant parts being;

1. Terumat hamaaser is a Hebrew term that means "tithe of the tithe".
2. Maaser Rishon is a term that refers to the first tithe.
3. Maaser Sheni and Maaser Ani are terms that refer to additional tithes.

Here is the mystery of God's hire unveiled

The original word for tithing is just that; ma'aser which is noun that means "a tenth part".

The tithe is not spiritually declared as God's portion. The whole tithe; but only the high tithe or the tenth part of the tithe that is due to the clergy overseer (Terumat hamaaser) It is the portion of the servant of the altar but the tithe did contain the unhallowed things. Meaning for it to be a set portion of God the high tithe should only contain the hallowed and choice things of the children of God; as the first lump that makes the heave offerings or the tithe of Israel holy.

Though there are a number of groupings regarding tithes; there are actually just three classifications of tithes:

1. The High Tithe (Tithe Of Tithes)
2. Holy Tithe (Levites Tithes)
3. Festival Tithe (Tithe of the kraal)

THE HIGH TITHE

The high tithe or tithes is the portion of tithe that is most holy; as it is a portion of the one who stand before God's children as a way finder for the people; it is for the Setman. The one who is in charge of the mission and vision of the chosen congregation of old or now. This portion of tithe is not exacted from the church but the priest and church workers. Of the tithe taken from the church; the pastoral team separate only the hallowed things unto the Setman as his portion of the tithe; only ten percent made only of the hallowed things.

This is not the portion that goes to the care of the congregation; but the portion of approach or Order. It is the portion given to the Setman as the one who the vision and mission of God speaks through. One intricate example being of Aaron and Moses.

Aaron and Moses

One perfect example being of Aaron and Moses; God gave Moses the place of the Setman for the purpose of leading Israel out of Egypt to Canaan. Moses of his own consent said he would not be able to fulfill.

Exodus 4:10-14 KJV *And Moses said unto the LORD, O my Lord, I am not eloquent, neither heretofore, nor since thou hast spoken unto thy servant: but I am slow of speech, and of a slow tongue. And the LORD said unto him, Who hath made man's mouth? Or who maketh the dumb, or deaf, or the seeing, or the blind? Have not I the LORD? Now therefore go, and I will be with thy mouth, and teach thee what thou shalt say. And he said, O my Lord, send, I pray thee, by the hand of him whom thou wilt send. And the anger of the LORD was kindled against Moses, and he said, Is not Aaron the Levite thy brother? I know that he can speak well. And also, behold, he cometh forth to meet thee: and when he seeth thee, he will be glad in his heart.*

A thing that made God raise a Setman in his place; so that Moses as God speaks through his servants may speak through Aaron. The arrangement making Moses no longer a Setman but a 'god' unto Aaron and Aaron in his stead being the Setman.

Exodus 4:15-16 KJV *And thou shalt speak unto him, and put words in his mouth: and I will be with thy mouth, and with his mouth, and will teach you what ye shall do. And he shall be thy spokesman unto the people: and he shall be, even he shall be to thee instead of a mouth, and thou shalt be to him instead of God.*

Exodus 4:15-16 BBE *Let him give ear to your voice, and you will put my words in his mouth; and I will be with your mouth and with his, teaching you what you have to do. And he will do the talking for you to the people: he will be to you as a mouth and you will be to him as God.*

God Himself did relinquish His place before Aaron so that Moses may take the place of God in Aaron's life. The ideal being; Moses had been trained forty years in a priest's house; being his father in law Jethro. Aaron was not just naïve but also having been a slave all his life; he could not be decisive having been dependable or driven to do any and much duty in his life. So, God for the sake of the authority of that forty years bestowed on Moses; He of His consent makes Moses God over Aaron; or He places Moses in the place of God in Aaron's life. A thing that obviously Aaron did not know as he soon purloined with Moses weighing himself an equal owed mostly to the ideal that he was the younger of his siblings being Aaron and Mariam.

Exodus 3:1 KJV *Now Moses kept the flock of Jethro his father in law, the* **Priest** *of Midian: and he led the flock to the backside of the desert, and came to the mountain of God, even to Horeb.*

The forty years of Moses observing Jethro serve at the altar could not be overlooked. Thus Moses was no longer the Setman but the "God" above Aaron instead of a Mediator. Understanding that, the dues of a Setman is no longer due to Moses. For in the Mosaic Law Moses did not stand as man but a 'God' over Aaron who stood as Setman in the place of Moses because he said he was not eloquent enough to lead. In simple terms, the addition of Aaron displaced both Moses and God. God became the exalted God to Israel, then Moses the immediate 'God' and then Aaron the Highpriest. That is why the Law is now called the Mosaic Law. For it is Moses speaking instead of God over the priesthood of the day. They are just handy men in the crafting and artifice of Moses. As Moses is the only one who can meet and converse with God, Moses is instead of God to them. They have to hear Moses to hear or no word from God could override Moses' 'Godship'.

So, the dues of Moses then are given to Aaron who stand in his stead; as the Setman or Highpriest. Making Moses stand over Israel instead of a Setman rather now as a judge. Meaning he is set beyond the office of the clergyman or man of the cloth; rather standing as the standard of perfection or an overseer beyond the office of a Highpriest. Being an obvious change in order (for further reading can read the book; **Order Ethic** by same author)

Numbers 18:25-29 KJV *And the LORD spake unto Moses, saying, Thus speak unto the Levites, and say unto them, When ye take of the children of Israel the tithes which I have given you from them for your inheritance, then ye shall offer up* *an heave offering of it for the LORD, even a tenth part of the tithe. And this your heave offering shall be reckoned unto you, as though it were the corn of the threshingfloor, and as the fulness of the winepress. Thus ye also shall offer an heave offering unto the LORD of all your tithes, which ye receive of the children of Israel; and ye shall give thereof the LORD'S heave offering to Aaron the priest. Out of all your gifts ye shall offer every heave offering of the LORD, of all the best thereof, even the hallowed part thereof out of it.*

Numbers 18:8, 11, 19-20 KJV *And the LORD spake unto Aaron, Behold, I also have given thee the charge of mine heave offerings of all the hallowed things of the children of Israel; unto thee have I given them by reason of the anointing, and to thy sons, by an ordinance for ever. And this is thine; the heave offering of their gift, with all the wave offerings of the children of Israel: I have given them unto thee, and to thy sons and to thy daughters with thee, by a statute for ever: every one that is clean in thy house shall eat of it. All the heave offerings of the holy things, which the children of Israel offer unto the LORD, have I given thee, and thy sons and thy daughters with thee, by a statute for ever: it is a covenant of salt for ever before the LORD unto thee and to thy seed with thee. And the LORD spake unto Aaron, Thou shalt have no inheritance in their land, neither shalt thou have any part among them: I am thy part and thine inheritance among the children of Israel.*

The above two sets of scripture separate two things. The heave offerings of the tithe and the other heave offerings of Israel. Only the heave offerings of the tithe or the high tithe or the tithe of tithes is secluded to Aaron being the Setman. And all the other heave offerings are for Aaron and his children. This is of uttermost importance to separate clearly.

The portion of Aaron or the portion of the Setman in the church is considered God's portion. Not just in the tithe of tithes but as also in the other heave offerings of the church. Yet only the tithe of tithes is for Aaron only. Meaning the high tithe was and is never set out for the workers at the altar but is given to the Setman because of the anointing or making of the vision and mission carrier of the congregation. He takes instead of God. It is not the whole tithe but the tithe of tithes that sanctifies it all. Then when the pastors and workers have the tithe in their courts it is to pass on the oil of the sanctified portion of their tithe to the sanctified portion of the tithe of the church or in the old of Israel.

THE TITHE

There is a thing that often escapes our hold as teachers of the word; more especially in tone and delivery when mentioning the dues. To any and all's surprise the dues or tithe is just classified as an offering though compulsory and not forgivable but rather only redemptive/redeemable at a charge of a fifth of its value more on top of the owed sum.

The high tithe and the common tithe has one simple thing that separates them being; the high tithe is only a tithe of the hallowed things and the Levites tithes are made of what remains after exacting God's portion from the tithe of the church. So, they come by bundled together and it is the work of the Levites to separate them and choose the best of the first tenth to the Setman then what is left of the heave offerings of Israel; or the tithe of Israel.

Numbers 18:21-24 UKJV *And, behold, I have given the children of Levi all the tenth in Israel for an inheritance, for their service which they serve, even the service of the tabernacle of the congregation. Neither must the children of Israel henceforth come nigh the tabernacle of the congregation, lest they bear sin, and die. But the Levites shall do the service of the tabernacle of the congregation, and they shall bear their iniquity: it shall be a statute for ever throughout your generations, that among the children of Israel they have no inheritance. But the tithes of the children of Israel, which they offer as an heave offering unto the LORD, I have given to the Levites to inherit: therefore I have said unto them, Among the children of Israel they shall have no inheritance.*

In simple terms after the treasury or tithe is collected. The first tenth part of the hallowed things is taken from it. It is the tithe of the pastors to the Highpriest; then whatever remains after taking out the lot that is God and given to the Setman. Then what remains is called tithes of the church and is due to the pastors and church workers as their pay.

FESTIVAL TITHE

The festival Tithe is usually scantily classified as the tithe of the kraal it is that part of tithe that is ascribed to the children of Israel to offer its part in burnt offering and the most part of it to others around them.

The tithe of the kraal is still a due in the church and has to be remembered for what it is worth. The ability to distribute it among the many about you freely. A thing that makes it a feasting tithe as the poor and the fatherless get a handful to sup their souls through out the season. Though it is not usually commonly talked about; the festival Tithe or the portion of tithe that is due to the poor; as the Levite at our gate; or serving us. It is a festive giving away where most of the tithe of the kraal is offered.

"Clinically" expounding tithe teaches us that it was set aside to provide not just for the worker and the Highpriest; but also the needy, the widow and the fatherless. It was more than a means to pay the work staff of God. It was a self sufficient way to provide and stand security for those who are not able to provide for self among the children of Israel. Israel being an agrarian society one may say it comes as a surprise that any would suffer lack; Christ confessed it even through His mouth that we shall always have the poor among us meaning poverty like offence is more than just a condition but at times even a spirit.

Mark 14:3-9 KJV *And being in Bethany in the house of Simon the leper, as he sat at meat, there came a woman having an alabaster box of ointment of spikenard very precious; and she brake the box, and poured it on his head. And there were some that had indignation within themselves, and said, Why was this waste of the ointment made? For it might have been* *sold for more than three hundred pence, and have been given to the poor. And they murmured against her. And Jesus said, Let her alone; why trouble ye her? She hath wrought a good work on me. For ye have the poor with you always, and whensoever ye will ye may do them good: but me ye have not always. She hath done what she could: she is come aforehand to anoint my body to the burying. Verily I say unto you, Wheresoever this gospel shall be preached throughout the whole world, this also that she hath done shall be spoken of for a memorial of her.*

So, the tithe was beneficial in the above three ways being a constant source of upkeep for those who have left their all to serve God as much as the feeble of the flock of God.

Tithe and Medieval English

Contrary to popular believe or strange as it might be. Tithe as heard to have evolved from an old English noun born of West Germanic number system of the number ten. Strange as it may seem; was not communalized by the Jewish or Judaic Covenant. It was popularized and first institutionalized by the English adaption of the faith. It is not in part but in all fullness an influence born of the English isles. The influence did not just spin the clergy's ways but even influenced English society; how they dispersed their land and many other reforms. The English and its royalty did take the ways of the cross a bit far too serious than any other peoples one would say.

A thing that shows not just by their medieval inclusion but the intrusion of it on to any colony they set. They went out carrying a gun and a bottle of brandy in one hand the Holy Bible in another. The English did not just advocate but did translate the much of their works in to the languages of the people they occupied; both the word and hymn books alike they did engage and set sure missions that stand Africa over to this day.

The English's influence in tithing did build astounding structures the world over. It birthed a renaissance of the ability of a well guarded and excited levy for it employed men during the 1600s as there were the king's men there were also the clergy men dedicated at executing the tithing system. One such men being William Shakespeare the common playwright. He did not just observe and paid but in the latter days of his life when he had rested the pen he did take to God's work in this respect; collecting tithe. A thing that would not come as a surprise as massive church buildings were built across Europe in the era and tithe had for a while even endured as part of common law to enforce building and providing for the clergy men and their assistants.

William Shakespeare do not just have been believed to have once been the Lord's Chamberlin but has even have the insinuation of tithe a number of times in his writings some being as follows;

1. "tithed" in Timon of Athens
2. "tithe-pig's tail" in Romeo and Juliet

3. "tithe's to sow" in Measure for Measure
4. "tithe-woman" in All's Well That Ends Well
5. "tithing" in King Lear

Tithe did not just endure in the English isles temporally but one would be keen to soon mention. Even the people who saw through the renaissance like Martin Luther King did support and endorse tithing when they restructured and rearrange the works of the Holy Bible. A thing that means the roots of tithe and the English has a long history not just spanning the missions era but also the restructuring and the indulgence of King James and some other royals in his linage. The word does not just take root of the English but has shaped their sphere as through tithe as commonly enforced and as a contemptible law did they do use the verb as the noun.

So, the definition of tithe can not be concluded without a clear mention of the English. A thing that expressly tells us why they so engaged in the missions works during the colonial era. They already had a sure tithing system that did not just distribute to the clergy but means beyond their realm. A thing that made missionary work as of old always engage a guy with and English name. A thing they did passionately and even of necessity by enforcement and even as a law of the land. An effort that did make them elaborate and farfetched among their peers. They did not take over the world by force but by the spreading of the words of peace as men emphasizing the need of a duplicate system of what the tithing in their land has made them become.

This is the part of the English people that is often forgotten. They rode in to conquer by peace; a thing that saved nations like Botswana to have never been colonized; the advise of the missions reaching their isles. So, by someone's tithe they did not just colonize but even preserved some peoples.

The Church's Usual Approach

The church's usual mistake.

The church's usual mistake is when they give cars or huge gifts to the man of God is when they are doing God service. No! God is a God of principle and He is not the author of chaos nor confusion. God has rather proved by all means to be self sufficient and had set the church to grow and become by being a self sufficient organism. The living church as the body of Christ was designed to have means that are balanced and elevated beyond some's reach. Where things seem unproportioned or lacking; it calls for questioning. Questioning not God but the execution of the ways or principles of God in that given church.

If the attention of the servant of God for example is set by God to be bought by cars and lavish gifts as it is the common thought of the new church. Then God has set an astounding trap for the feeble and lacking among the church his flock. They simplistically will never be able to receive much or move the heart of God. And in that setting where God rewards the privileged only by their enabled effort: what shall be the portion of the poor and those unable to purchase him/her?

An astounding question though some how rushed and too fore mentioned for now. Until you understand exactly how the Setman of any congregation should be supported and provided for, you miss the ideal of how much unworthy damage those who go all out in an effort to provoke the anointing upon the head of the man of God do put to waste as it is a common thing to buy one's way in to the inner circle. A thing that even cause some to go and borrow what they do not have to lay upon the altar of God: God never requires what He has never given you by principle. He would never require money that you have not acquired nor take what is not yours and expects you to pay by a sudden turn of events.

Faith though often mentioned is soon mocked.

Soon mocked because it is not applied according to principle and so happens to be the care of the servant of God. A thing that often cause bias for most give or sow in to him for show and to heave his attention unproportioned untoward the church but to a certain well to do individuals. So the more the provision for the Setman the more chaos and hurt is dished the undiscerning. A thing that means they would often give in to a man when they think they are giving in to God.

Luke 14:12-24 KJV *Then said he also to him that bade him, When thou makest a dinner or a supper, call not thy friends, nor thy brethren, neither thy kinsmen, nor thy rich neighbours; lest they also bid thee again, and a recompence be made thee. But when thou makest a feast, call the poor, the maimed, the lame, the blind: And thou shalt be blessed; for they cannot recompense thee: for thou shalt be recompensed at the resurrection of the just. And when one of them that sat at* *meat with him heard these things, he said unto him, Blessed is he that shall eat bread in the kingdom of God. Then said he unto him, A certain man made a great supper, and bade many: And sent his servant at supper time to say to them that were bidden, Come; for all things are now ready. And they all with one consent began to make excuse. The first said unto him, I have bought a piece of ground, and I must needs go and see it: I pray thee have me excused. And another said, I have bought five yoke of oxen, and I go to prove them: I pray thee have me excused. And another said, I have married a wife, and therefore I cannot come. So that servant came, and shewed his lord these things. Then the master of the house being angry said to his servant, Go out quickly into the streets and lanes of the city, and bring in hither the poor, and the maimed, and the halt, and the blind. And the servant said, Lord, it is done as thou hast commanded, and yet there is room. And the lord said unto the servant, Go out into the highways and hedges, and compel them to come in, that my house may be filled. For I say unto you, That none of those men which were bidden shall taste of my supper.*

The principle of sowing a seed is often misconstrued by many as they would always want to aim their seed at the man who has something to offer in return. A thing that means if the do not get desired attention back it back fires to their hurt and destruction. Rather Christ advise on sowing in to those who have no power or position to restitute or recompense. Then their reward shall not come from man but God. In that way your would be directed to God not a mediator among you.

In favor of self due to the intricate setting of the new church soon the servant of God points to self as the source and power that carries the anointing that releases the church's blessings. It is not so, in giving dues as they are supposed is the blessing of God set in his principle. As apostle Paul talked to the church in Macedonia Philippi about their consistency in the dues and offering by principle. A thing they saw to its distribution as Paul was by a change of order the assumptive Setman of the gentiles. They did owe to him the tithe of tithes from all the gentile churches but only a certain few did partake. A thing that often made him suffer up and downs according to his words.

Philippians 4:10-19 KJV *But I rejoiced in the Lord greatly, that now at the last your care of me hath flourished again; wherein ye were also careful, but ye lacked opportunity. Not that I speak in respect of want: for I have learned, in whatsoever state I am, therewith to be content. I know both how to be abased, and I know how to abound: every where and in all things I am instructed both to be full and to be hungry, both to abound and to suffer need. I can do all things through Christ which strengtheneth me. Notwithstanding ye have well done, that ye did communicate with my affliction. Now ye Philippians know also, that in the beginning of the gospel, when I departed from Macedonia, no church communicated with me as concerning giving and receiving, but ye only. For even in Thessalonica ye sent once and again unto my necessity. Not because I desire a gift: but I desire fruit that may abound to your account. But I have all, and abound: I am full, having received of Epaphroditus the things which were sent from you, an odour of a sweet smell, a sacrifice acceptable, wellpleasing to God. But my God shall supply all your need according to his riches in glory by Christ Jesus.*

Usually when one hears Paul saying the region of Philippi has flourished again. They miss his interpretation of the condition of the Philippians who obvious suffered lack for a while and there was a draught of resources so failed to reach him with their lot but when restored were quick to fill in their spot. It does not mean random gifting but the portion set for his accord and office as general overseer of the gentile church. A thing that he soon touches regarding the church at Corinth; that he is receiving wages from other churches to do them service.

2 Corinthians 11:7-12 KJV *Have I committed an offence in abasing myself that ye might be exalted, because I have preached to you the gospel of God freely? I robbed other churches, taking wages of them, to do you service. And when I was present with you, and wanted, I was chargeable to no man: for that which was lacking to me the brethren which came from Macedonia supplied: and in all things I have kept myself from being burdensome unto you, and so will I keep myself. As the truth of Christ is in me, no man shall stop me of this boasting in the regions of Achaia. Wherefore? Because I love you not? God knoweth. But what I do, that I will do, that I may cut off occasion from them which desire occasion; that wherein they glory, they may be found even as we.*

One would soon ask; then what is the wage of the set man?

Is he not supposed to be provided for by sowing seeds or love offerings?

Of course love or heave offering can in all gladness be given to the Setman and his household as appreciation gifts but what is the true pay of the set man in church one has to be sure in order to serve accordingly not by bias. Not by guilt and not by feeling ashamed.

So, the modern church is mostly taught that by providing or sowing in to the man of God shall prosper them but the word does not say so. The word simply says the church is provided for by entering in at the door that is Christ. Simply put; being truly introduced to Christ and taking Him up for self.

John 10:7-9 KJV *Then said Jesus unto them again, Verily, verily, I say unto you, I am the door of the sheep. All that ever came before me are thieves and robbers: but the sheep did not hear them. I am the door: by me if any man enter in, he shall be saved, and shall go in and out, and find pasture.*

This simply shows us, by offering to a certain person but Jesus Christ's will does not edify but rather robs the giver as Christ gives the example of the priesthood that came before him. That sowing in to a man of authority as in a fellow human you do not reap but are rather robbed. The below scripture is often confused that though it is a continuation of the above word talking about the priesthood or pastors is often misinterpreted as to Christ referring to the devil. It is a continuation of the former portion of scripture which defines the robbers and thieves who came before Christ being the Levitical priesthood.

John 10:10-18 KJV *The thief cometh not, but for to steal, and to kill, and to destroy: I am come that they might have life, and that they might have it more abundantly. I am the good shepherd: the good shepherd giveth his life for the sheep. But he that is an hireling, and not the shepherd, whose own the sheep are not, seeth the wolf coming, and leaveth the sheep, and fleeth: and the wolf catcheth them, and scattereth the sheep. The hireling fleeth, because he is an hireling, and careth not for the sheep. I am the good shepherd, and know my sheep, and am known of mine. As the Father knoweth me, even so know I the Father: and I lay down my life for the sheep. And other sheep I have, which are not of this fold: them also I must bring, and they shall hear my voice; and there shall be one fold, and one shepherd. Therefore doth my Father love me, because I lay down my life, that I might take it again. No man taketh it from me, but I lay it down of myself. I have power to lay it down, and I have power to take it again. This commandment have I received of my Father.*

The above words talks about the priest by hire of the man of cloth not the devil. That though he stands in the lot of God, he does not have the power to give life to the sheep but to refer them to the door. Or otherwise it is to the damage or robbing of the sheep. Yet if he is a hireling: what is his hire or wage?

Definitely a thing that would surely call him a thief if when he has collected from his Master he would require seed of the flock. That would prove him insatiable, as when he has his lot by right should not lure the flock in to giving him/her extra money to enrich self and over exact what is due to him. A thing that John the Baptist openly shunned.

Luke 3:12-14 KJV *Then came also publicans to be baptized, and said unto him, Master, what shall we do? And he said unto them, Exact no more than that which is appointed you. And the soldiers likewise demanded of him, saying, And what shall we do? And he said unto them, Do violence to no man, neither accuse any falsely; and be content with your wages.*

Meaning the occurrence of the random seeking of seed is a sign of a malady. A thing that seek occasion on the one to be pried with deceit yet how do we know it is not right to set one in the place of the provider if Christ says providence is in entering by the door; that is according to Him it is not in being laid hands upon or being prayed for. Then how come the Setman often openly expresses the ideal that the things of the church are in him or her.

Is it starvation or an innocent contradiction?

Once you understand the lot afforded the Setman then if he by any means ask for more; it is both deceit and fallacy a thing that means the church has to question herself if they are doing their part to afford the Setman his hire or do they even know what is the Setman's hire? A thing then that would mean they are probably robbing the Setman in turn turning the same scripture against themselves as did God against Israel in the book of Malachi.

Malachi 3:5-12 KJV *And I will come near to you to judgment; and I will be a swift witness against the sorcerers, and against the adulterers, and against false swearers, and against those that oppress the hireling in his wages, the widow, and the fatherless, and that turn aside the stranger from his right, and fear not me, saith the LORD of hosts. For I am the LORD, I change not; therefore ye sons of Jacob are not consumed. Even from the days of your fathers ye are gone away from mine ordinances, and have not kept them. Return unto me, and I will return unto you, saith the LORD of hosts. But ye said, Wherein shall we return? Will a man rob God? Yet ye have robbed me. But ye say, Wherein have we robbed thee? In tithes and offerings. Ye are cursed with a curse: for ye have robbed me, even this whole nation. Bring ye all the tithes into the storehouse, that there may be meat in mine house, and prove me now herewith, saith the LORD of hosts, if I will not open you the windows of heaven, and pour you out a blessing, that there shall not be room enough to receive it. And I will rebuke the devourer for your sakes, and he shall not destroy the fruits of your ground; neither shall your vine cast her fruit before the time in the field, saith the LORD of hosts. And all nations shall call you blessed: for ye shall be a delightsome land, saith the LORD of hosts.*

In the above scripture God talks about Israel oppressing the hireling by not giving him his hire. Then He goes on to talk about robbing Him. A challenge that means if you know the dues of the Setman you should be swift to give him his dues before he is tempted to do satiate self otherwise.

This calls for a real word search. For if as it already proves contrary that the Setman says your providence is in him and Christ says it is in entering in at the door. Then we are at diametric; diametric that could of an astounding discovery. The discovering that one has been pour their things in to a sack without a bottom. If all the promises of the Setman do not hold enough evidence or water to be true when reflected through Christ who is the author and the finisher of our faith. A thing that truly takes back to **John 10:10**; being killed, stolen from and destroyed by those that come after Christ now.

A Tithe Of Tithes

Why the **Tithe Of Tithes**?

The **Tithe Of Tithes** is a sure measure that will enable the Setman to take care of the whole church accordingly. In simple terms every branch has to contribute to the welfare and expansion of the church as one and a tithe of tithes removes all bias. As the Lord has provided according to one's setting; so the Lord will proportionally take from all among His children to provide for His servant whom He has directly set and ordained for the purpose of raising a certain church by a certain mission and vision.

So to be able to give a blanketing or wholly covering effort; he has to be provided for to do just that. So, the ten percent of the church's tithe is a secure and sure value that can enable him to do that despite the distance and the broadness of the work. It provides rest and surety and destroys bias in the service and judgement of the servant of God. A thing that would soon destroy the brewing ill of the servant of God being provided for by a certain group of people; often not by merit or because they are born of God. Meaning the work of God is being taken care of by the enemy making it the work of the enemy. For these have to as often as they give be heaved before the church in acknowledgement or be well placed in the church by the accord of their means. A thing often done in-kind by pushing them to offices and places of influence so that they can be spent and spend with the assurance that it is done for them and with their added contribution in decision making.

It makes the church respecters of persons; a thing so unashamedly done by the new church and often displayed unashamedly by having men who are not born of God placed well in His church whereas His children are stuffed about. It is a pity that the church now our days have VIP and even VIPP as men not born of God; but men who have booked their seats with money for consultation aimed at enriching one man; being the set man.

James 2:1-9 KJV *My brethren, have not the faith of our Lord Jesus Christ, the Lord of glory, with respect of persons. For if there come unto your assembly a man with a gold ring, in goodly apparel, and there come in also a poor man in vile raiment; And ye have respect to him that weareth the gay clothing, and say unto him, Sit thou here in a good place; and say to the poor, Stand thou there, or sit here under my footstool: Are ye not then partial in yourselves, and are become judges of evil thoughts? Hearken, my beloved brethren, Hath not God chosen the poor of this world rich in faith, and heirs of the kingdom which he hath promised to them that love him? But ye have despised the poor. Do not rich men oppress you, and draw you before the judgment seats? Do not they blaspheme that worthy name by the which ye are called? If ye fulfil the royal law according to the scripture, Thou shalt love thy neighbour as thyself, ye do well: But if ye have respect to persons, ye commit sin, and are convinced of the law as transgressors.*

One has to carefully study these things; that now it is the proud and arrogant of this world that are afforded a chance and are given the first privilege and a place to benefit of the riches of God's glory before His children. Only they have money strings to pull and there dances men of God. And they are sure and set in themselves that they have the right to draw the servant of God with cords often of deception. As they are the church financiers.

So, the tithe of tithes gives the servant of God unbiased ability to serve accordingly and live to a certain standard that does not make him or her depend on individuals but rather the work of God. Dealing away with imbalances for the sake of milking the certain well-offs of the church who in turn do keep the front row not only of the church but even access and denial of reaching the pastor; whether they are truly faithful to God or not.

So, with the tithe of tithes drawn from the tithe of the whole church. It kills individualism and the demonstration of dominance by any means. Making it a joint effort rather than a thing born of a certain individual. Causing the servant of God no extra pressure to prove sure any certain individual or group in association or in-kind to hold them around him as the ones buttering his bread. So turning him to be possessive and protective of a certain group of individuals over others.

The Setman and the overseer. At times the Setman is confused for the overseer but it is not so. The Setman is the man appointed by God and given a mission and vision and a name for a church to establish and lead. But the overseer can be anyone who has been interested in to the task of the bishopric. A thing that means there is a varied difference between the two.

That is why when Israel returns from the captivity in Babylon do gather the tithe of tithes and sum it up to be used as the provision for those stationed in the temple as it had been rebuilt.

Nehemiah 10:38-39 KJV *And the priest the son of Aaron shall be with the Levites, when the Levites take tithes: and the Levites shall bring up the tithe of the tithes unto the house of our God, to the chambers, into the treasure house. For the children of Israel and the children of Levi shall bring the offering of the corn, of the new wine, and the oil, unto the chambers, where are the vessels of the sanctuary, and the priests that minister, and the porters, and the singers: and we will not forsake the house of our God.*

One begins to see a change of order when Aaron is no longer the Highpriest but his children. Meaning whoever rose in his stead was no longer as Aaron was. They were a Highpriest and a overseer instead of a Highpriest and a Setman. Meaning they were in the stead of Aaron not by the reason of the anointing but by the linage of genealogy.

Numbers 18:8 KJV *And the LORD spake unto Aaron, Behold, I also have given thee the charge of mine heave offerings of all the hallowed things of the children of Israel; unto thee have I given them by reason of the anointing, and to thy sons, by an ordinance for ever.*

Governing Bias

One real important thing that any would acknowledge in any given modern church is an obvious bias when it comes to a certain family or group of people in relation with the man of God; the ideal being they are more like the church bread winners. Or one may correct self; they are more like the providers of the pastor or the Setman. It happens at all church levels, regarding the headquarters or the branch level. There are always those people or family that can get you to see the man of God almost instantaneously.

One simple thing that often brings in rot in to any given church is the pastor's lack and inadequacy when it comes to finances. God did provide the tithe of tithes to be a way to govern bias in church. When the man of God is well served and fed, he will by nature not be haughty of heart. So the portion that is set aside for him, it is to do govern his affairs in a reputable way. The ideal being his remuneration is drawn from the wholesomeness of the tithe not by the church members but by the pastoral team. A thing that means he would not make of it who offered what? A thing that comes with a bias of its own as it means if the servant of God knows who gave what would be forced by nature to be preferable when it comes to serving the flock.

The bias of course would always come as an example to exemplify what being merit at offering God would do in one's life. A thing that quickly corrupts hearts as soon everyone would be striving to please the servant rather than God. A thing so loathed by God; for the more power man tastes the corrupt he becomes.

Romans 1:20-32 KJV *For the invisible things of him from the creation of the world are clearly seen, being understood by the things that are made, even his eternal power and Godhead; so that they are without excuse: Because that, when they knew God, they glorified him not as God, neither were thankful; but became vain in their imaginations, and their foolish heart was darkened. Professing themselves to be wise, they became fools, And changed the glory of the uncorruptible God into an image made like to corruptible man, and to birds, and fourfooted beasts, and creeping things. Wherefore God also gave them up to uncleanness through the lusts of their own hearts, to dishonour their own bodies between themselves: Who changed the truth of God into a lie, and worshipped and served the creature more than the Creator, who is blessed for ever. Amen. For this cause God gave them up unto vile affections: for even their women did change the natural use into that which is against nature: And likewise also the men, leaving the natural use of the woman, burned in their lust one toward another; men with men working that which is unseemly, and receiving in themselves that recompence of their error which was meet. And even as they did not like to retain God in their knowledge, God gave them over to a reprobate mind, to do those* *things which are not convenient; Being filled with all unrighteousness, fornication, wickedness, covetousness, maliciousness; full of envy, murder, debate, deceit, malignity; whisperers, Backbiters, haters of God, despiteful, proud, boasters, inventors of evil things, disobedient to parents, Without understanding, covenantbreakers, without natural affection, implacable, unmerciful: Who knowing the judgment of God, that they which commit such things are worthy of death, not only do the same, but have pleasure in them that do them.*

So, whenever we honor each other instead of God who brought us together. We give dues to men because they are entitled; but when we honor God we do things by principle. Doing things by principle means we will direct all our efforts toward God, who in turn gives us His reward; not a man's reward. But godly reward as per His standard without bias.

Matthew 10:40-42 UKJV *He that receives you receives me, and he that receives me receives him that sent me. He that receives a prophet in the name of a prophet shall receive a prophet's reward; and he that receives a righteous man in the name of a righteous man shall receive a righteous man's reward. And whosoever shall give to drink unto one of these little ones a cup of cold water only in the name of a disciple, verily I say unto you, he shall in no wise lose his reward.*

There is a thing that is often missed in the above scripture. When it says when you receive a righteous man because he is righteous; you receive a righteous man's reward. It means you receive from the man or the prophet not from God. People are generally excited when they hear you shall receive a prophet's reward. Yet they do not consider why Christ mentions Himself first then the prophet and the righteous man. It is because whatever you receive from man is manly and earthly and full of bias. Meaning it is not from God.

A thing that means we should be doing what is principled by Christ to receive of Him rather than of men.

Mark 9:41 KJV *For whosoever shall give you a cup of water to drink in my name, because ye belong to Christ, verily I say unto you, he shall not lose his reward.*

Keeping Order

Where there is no bias there is a perfect order in rank and everything. But when bias creeps in, the wrong people are set on spots undeserving of their character or abilities; a thing that means order escapes the matters of the congregation for the naïve privileged would soon prove to be as babes toying with things of the mature. It takes both heart and patience to work the work of God and as much sincerely should take much dedication to care for those who have their lives to labor in the spirit and the care and the welfare of the church.

The duty of care on its own is lonesome.

So, the separatism the servant of God suffers in laboring in prayers and fasting deserves a due recompense timely here on earth. A thing that on its own eats of order. Meaning, if tithe is not collected by the relevant scripted person's according to scripture there is a due catastrophe impending the church. The church board and elective committee members are often people not elected by right but rite. A thing that means customarily the church would look for someone they trust to have money and things that he/she can be liable to return the lost things Incase of any mishap or misuse. A thing that means committees are characterized by people who hold an earthly position with some form of responsibility that can on its own hinder the collection and reimbursing of both the church worker as the Setman. Naturally the work of God comes as second string by design.

So biblically it is the work of the pastoral team to collect the tithe and to do choose the best and hallowed first tenth of it for the Setman. A thing that carries a due sensitivity by the one who is in the office by call and not by bias or rite. So, as it is scripted it often fights the regulatory authorities but one has to pen it down and support it with scripture why it has to be done that way in their constitution. A thing that would preserve order and timeous delivery of the dues.

Numbers 18:20-32 KJV *And the LORD spake unto Aaron, Thou shalt have no inheritance in their land, neither shalt thou have any part among them: I am thy part and thine inheritance among the children of Israel. And, behold, I have given the children of Levi all the tenth in Israel for an inheritance, for their service which they serve, even the service of the tabernacle of the congregation. Neither must the children of Israel henceforth come nigh the tabernacle of the congregation, lest they bear sin, and die. But the Levites shall do the service of the tabernacle of the congregation, and they shall bear their iniquity: it shall be a statute for ever throughout your generations, that among the children of Israel they have no inheritance. But the tithes of the children of Israel, which they offer as an heave offering unto the LORD, I have given to the Levites to inherit: therefore I have said unto them, Among the children of Israel they shall have no inheritance. And the LORD spake unto Moses, saying, Thus speak unto the Levites, and say unto them, When ye take of the children of Israel the tithes which I have given you from them for your inheritance, then ye shall offer up an heave offering of it for the LORD, even a tenth part of the tithe. And this your heave offering shall be reckoned unto you, as though it were the corn of the threshingfloor, and as the fulness of the winepress. Thus ye also shall offer an heave offering unto the LORD of all your tithes, which ye receive of the children of Israel; and ye shall give thereof the LORD'S heave offering to Aaron the priest. Out of all your gifts ye shall offer every heave offering of the LORD, of all the best thereof, even the hallowed part thereof out of it. Therefore thou shalt say unto them, When ye have heaved the best thereof from it, then it shall be counted unto the Levites as the increase of the threshingfloor, and as the increase of the winepress. And ye shall eat it in every place, ye and your households: for it is your* *reward for your service in the tabernacle of the congregation. And ye shall bear no sin by reason of it, when ye have heaved from it the best of it: neither shall ye pollute the holy things of the children of Israel, lest ye die.*

Crushing Sectarism

Sectarism is often born of ideologies. A thing that means any can rise where there is no outline of how things are done.

One would ask; where in the New Testament does the Holy Bible talk about tithe of tithes?

Where apostle Paul attest to have been collecting wages from the churches. It means as the one given the gentiles church as the assumptive Setman; he by rite do not take the whole tithe from other churches because there were deacons and bishops stationed in those places. By default he was taking a tithe of the tithes; so that the bishops and deacons may be maintained by the tithe. An order he naturally knew as a schooled servant trained the way of things of God. He knew how the overseer is provided for and how the church worker and pastor are provided for. It means by natural design he knew the transference of pastors in to the New Testament; transfers the burdens of their care to the New Testament. A thing that means whosoever serves at the altar is a partaker of the things of the said altar by reason of being spent for that altar.

2 Corinthians 11:8-9 KJV *I robbed other churches, taking wages of them, to do you service. And when I was present with you, and wanted, I was chargeable to no man: for that which was lacking to me the brethren which came from Macedonia supplied: and in all things I have kept myself from being burdensome unto you, and so will I keep myself.*

Naturally when Christ transferred the office of the pastor from the Old Testament congregation to the New Testament congregation. He of necessity had to transfer also their hire or else He has authored confusion in the church. For it would mean then anyone and everyone can decide how the Setman is remunerated and how the pastor is paid by their own desire and feelings. A thing that would mean Christ introduced Sectarism in to the church of God. So, when He says I will choose pastors according to my heart; He also has their providence at heart. The Setman as the pastor and the church worker.

So, if any would stand to contest. One would ask; if they are to be spent, how shall they be rewarded; even Christ Himself told them not to charge anyone anything but only take the worth of their work. That is why He told them to not take anything extra of their own; for the gospel already had a way. A way to sustain self through the dues chargeable to the church not the masses. The holy portion can only be exacted of those who are right and perfect before God. That is why He sends them and charges them not to charge the world out there; because they were received freely and received freely and they had to bring them in freely and without an external charge.

Matthew 10:7-11 KJV *And as ye go, preach, saying, The kingdom of heaven is at hand. Heal the sick, cleanse the lepers, raise the dead, cast out devils: freely ye have received, freely give. Provide neither gold, nor silver, nor brass in your purses, Nor scrip for your journey, neither two coats, neither shoes, nor yet staves: for the workman is worthy of his meat. And into whatsoever city or town ye shall enter, enquire who in it is worthy; and there abide till ye go thence.*

Usually when people hear; freely you have received freely give; they jumped in to conclusion; the pastor should not be paid. They do not look first at what leads to that statement. Jesus Christ does not tell the apostles to just enter any where: He says they should first ask if the person is worthy or right with God. Is it a person who pays their dues and keep the way of God; yes. Then use that person's substance because they belong to the kingdom; you are only a burden to the saved not the world. For you are a gift only to the church of God. Then take nothing of the world; just give them freely for freely you have received the abilities of the sonship of God. It is the due to the world or the unsaved Israel that Christ talked about; He wanted them to accept nothing from the strayed of Israel. Just help them find the way first. It was for the mission that they went to fulfill. A call for one who goes doing soul winning; do not charge anyone you go out to win back to God. That was the message they took for the road trip and it was not a pastoral order to the church.

Jeremiah 3:15-16 KJV *And I will give you pastors according to mine heart, which shall feed you with knowledge and understanding. And it shall come to pass, when ye be multiplied and increased in the land, in those days, saith the LORD, they shall say no more, The ark of the covenant of the LORD: neither shall it come to mind: neither shall they remember it; neither shall they visit it; neither shall that be done any more.*

Apostle Paul himself upon the words of Christ do add to the cost of the labors of serving as deserving of a pay; as someone would warring for a set kingdom for a set reward.

1 Corinthians 9:4-14 KJV *Have we not power to eat and to drink? Have we not power to lead about a sister, a wife, as well as other apostles, and as the brethren of the Lord, and Cephas? Or I only and Barnabas, have not we power to forbear working? Who goeth a warfare any time at his own charges? Who planteth a vineyard, and eateth not of the fruit thereof? Or who feedeth a flock, and eateth not of the milk of the flock? Say I these things as a man? Or saith not the law the same also? For it is written in the law of Moses, Thou shalt not muzzle the mouth of the ox that treadeth out the corn. Doth God take care for oxen? Or saith he it altogether for our sakes? For our sakes, no doubt, this is written: that he that ploweth should plow in hope; and that he that thresheth in hope should be partaker of his hope. If we have sown unto you spiritual things, is it a great thing if we shall reap your carnal things? If others be partakers of this power over you, are not we rather? Nevertheless we have not used this power; but suffer all things, lest we should hinder the gospel of Christ. Do ye not know that they which minister about holy things live of the things of the temple? And they which wait at the altar are partakers with the altar? Even so hath the Lord ordained that they which preach the gospel should live of the gospel.*

So, without the said limit of the tithe of tithes; even the Setman is at liberty to defraud as he does not have a measure governing his ways. One thing one soon picks of Apostle Peter as the Setman of the church of Christ at the beginning of the early church is that he did not indoctrinate and give a limit or monitor the giving and receiving according to principle. Christ literally left the church under his care as His chosen Setman out of the apostles. He was promised and later given the right to feed the church of Christ right there in the midst of the apostles. He was not taken aside but chosen in plain site.

John 21:15-17 KJV *So when they had dined, Jesus saith to Simon Peter, Simon, son of Jonas, lovest thou me more than these? He saith unto him, Yea, Lord; thou knowest that I love thee. He saith unto him, Feed my lambs. He saith to him again the second time, Simon, son of Jonas, lovest thou me? He saith unto him, Yea, Lord; thou knowest that I love thee. He saith unto him, Feed my sheep. He saith unto him the third time, Simon, son of Jonas, lovest thou me? Peter was grieved because he said unto him the third time, Lovest thou me? And he said unto him, Lord, thou knowest all things; thou knowest that I love thee. Jesus saith unto him, Feed my sheep.*

The first thing that Peter missed was the only thing he was instructed to do. To feed Christ's sheep with knowledge and understanding. Casting it in the teeth of the prophecy given through prophet Jeremiah.

Jeremiah 3:15-16 KJV *And I will give you pastors according to mine heart, which shall feed you with knowledge and understanding. And it shall come to pass, when ye be multiplied and increased in the land, in those days, saith the LORD, they shall say no more, The ark of the covenant of the LORD: neither shall it come to mind: neither shall they remember it; neither shall they visit it; neither shall that be done any more.*

He was swept off the feet by the tremendous amount of power ushered through him. And soon forgot why Christ did choose him from the twelve. And the thing that made sure the promise of Christ to set Peter as the Setman of His church. For who He met but a stone He did grow in to a rock and promised to build the foundations of His church upon him; being the Setman.

Matthew 16:18-19 KJV *And I say also unto thee, That thou art Peter, and upon this rock I will build my church; and the gates of hell shall not prevail against it. And I will give unto thee the keys of the kingdom of heaven: and whatsoever thou shalt bind on earth shall be bound in heaven: and whatsoever thou shalt loose on earth shall be loosed in heaven.*

As Moses' first miracle done when not under pressure committed him to a limitation to not enter the land of promise; so the helm made Peter forget. All the open rebukes he suffered from Christ and the much induction as the Lord's right hand man went the way of the window. A thing that ends up leading him to kill Sapphira and Ananias; because they did not openly give it all. They could discern the impending danger of giving away everything they had without any form of security or assurance from God. They would not just copy others and so they suffered for their wisdom. A thing that soon finds a church that was said to lack nothing being fundraised for by apostle Paul; by remembering the poor among them. One would say; what happened of the providence and sufficiency for all at the beginning. The things were spent and people fell back in to lack. A thing that caused him to collect ought even of the usually shunned church at Corinth and the soon riotous church at Galatia. To remember the poor at Jerusalem by a collection for the saints there.

The urgency of the collection tells one how dire it was for Paul to take anything from Corinth. He lived among them and would not take a thing from them; but for the sake of the saints in Jerusalem he had to write a wonderfully set poetic request to make them move for the need of the church of Christ in Jerusalem. It was not just unlike him; but absurd. Though often read for tithe and offerings collection; one would say it is definitely biased, a lure and a bribery to take from the usually left alone.

2 Corinthians 11:7-9 KJV *Have I committed an offence in abasing myself that ye might be exalted, because I have preached to you the gospel of God freely? I robbed other churches, taking wages of them, to do you service. And when I was present with you, and wanted, I was chargeable to no man: for that which was lacking to me the brethren which came from Macedonia supplied: and in all things I have kept myself from being burdensome unto you, and so will I keep myself.*

He did not just exact of Corinth but also the infamous Galatians for the sake of the poor of the church in Jerusalem. Another surprise for the sake of the saints in Jerusalem.

Galatians 2:10 KJV *Only they would that we should remember the poor; the same which I also was forward to do.*

1 Corinthians 16:1-3 KJV *Now concerning the collection for the saints, as I have given order to the churches of Galatia, even so do ye. Upon the first day of the week let every one of you lay by him in store, as God hath prospered him, that there be no gatherings when I come. And when I come, whomsoever ye shall approve by your letters, them will I send to bring your liberality unto Jerusalem.*

One would not just say the ways of Peter and the apostles did not just rob the church at Jerusalem but made them literal beggars though Paul did attempt the much to glorify and poetize the much the help they needed as a way for God to aid the churches. It was an adverse thing that he did even admonish the church at Corinth so kindly unlike at all other times where he did not take any sort of dues from them. But the lack of the church at Jerusalem did become a lament to all the gentile churches whereas the modern church is often taught they lacked nothing. One simple era; a lack of measure towards giving and receiving did make the church destitute. A thing that happened of King Solomon so did announce self to Jerusalem again. A thing that cause Paul to give the church at Corinth one of yet the most sang of verses when it comes to giving and receiving. The absolute luring of the Holy Bible.

2 Corinthians 9:1-13 KJV *For as touching the ministering to the saints, it is superfluous for me to write to you: For I know the forwardness of your mind, for which I boast of you to them of Macedonia, that Achaia was ready a year ago; and your zeal hath provoked very many. Yet have I sent the brethren, lest our boasting of you should be in vain in this behalf; that, as I said, ye may be ready: Lest haply if they of Macedonia come with me, and find you unprepared, we (that we say not, ye) should be ashamed in this same confident boasting. Therefore I thought it necessary to exhort the brethren, that they would go before unto you, and make up beforehand your bounty, whereof ye had notice before, that the same might be ready, as a matter of bounty, and not as of covetousness. But this I say, He which soweth sparingly shall reap also sparingly; and he which soweth bountifully shall reap also bountifully. Every man according as he purposeth in his heart, so let him give; not grudgingly, or of necessity: for God loveth a cheerful giver. And God is able to make all grace abound toward you; that ye, always having all sufficiency in all things, may abound to every good work: (As it is written, He hath dispersed abroad; he hath given to the poor: his righteousness remaineth for ever. Now he that ministereth seed to the sower both minister bread for your food, and multiply your seed sown, and increase the fruits of your righteousness;) Being enriched in every thing to all bountifulness, which causeth through us thanksgiving to God. For the administration of this service not only supplieth the want of the saints, but is abundant also by many thanksgivings unto God; Whiles by the experiment of this ministration they glorify God for your professed subjection unto the gospel of Christ, and for your liberal distribution unto them, and unto all men;*

And the message was spread adoringly to all gentile churches at large.

Romans 15:25-29 KJV *But now I go unto Jerusalem to minister unto the saints. For it hath pleased them of Macedonia and Achaia to make a certain contribution for the poor saints which are at Jerusalem. It hath pleased them verily; and their debtors they are. For if the Gentiles have been made partakers of their spiritual things, their duty is also to minister unto them in carnal things. When therefore I have performed this, and have sealed to them this fruit, I will come by you into Spain. And I am sure that, when I come unto you, I shall come in the fulness of the blessing of the gospel of Christ.*

Curbs Trickery Of Hand By The Messenger

Lack can make even the most candid of men rather slippery.

One would tell you even the most honest of men would break if they are constantly burdened by lack. It gives birth to traitors and means of defrauding. A thing that one would say wide spread in what we currently call the church of God. The supposed men of God sell products by advocating for their power and worth rather than the faith in Christ. Christ does not say you have to have hands laid on you or buy any form of oil or product to get a job and providence in your life. It is all in knowing Him and choosing Him; period.

The rest is fallacy and fallible vanities. Yet when you go everywhere there are vast promises that go with the promise of providence. A thing that means the servants of God are using other means to procure their lot from the church. The tithe of tithes was instated to curb such things. It is not just providence but security now and beyond the day of the office of pastor that bothers the man of the cloth.

What shall be life after this?

Though the truth be easy and straight forward; it is cluttered by the realities. That if one sticks to the truth, how shall they be provided for?

John 10:9 KJV *I am the door: by me if any man enter in, he shall be saved, and shall go in and out, and find pasture.*

Pasture as in the above scripture means providence. Where water would mean the Holy Spirit in the word. So, it is in coming into Christ that we get our providence. Not being under an anointed man of God or a prophet or any other thing. But the character of the church and often lack of foundational knowledge leads the pastor to sleight of hand.

The lack of an outlined pay for the Setman or pastor often leads them to such practices where they in an underlying way charge for services by other means. A thing that means they either swim the wrong way or sink by the way of the truth. Though Christ has with the simplest of ease elaborated that whoever enters by the door gets providence and rest and salvation; the preacher simply fails to say that in salvation there is the wholeness of providence. A thing that means the laying of hands would no longer be subjected to him and his profiteering as people usually are not kin to pay the dues.

It is not just the assumption of power by anointing but also the scarecrow that there are spirits that can only be addressed by a pastor; which is an utter lie. A devil is a devil and the name Jesus Christ is above them all; not the anointing but the name Jesus and all that are saved have enough power to deal with that. The pastor or the four fold ministry and the empty office are not raised for that; but the whole church.

Mark 16:17-18 KJV *And these signs shall follow them that believe; In my name shall they cast out devils; they shall speak with new tongues; They shall take up serpents; and if they drink any deadly thing, it shall not hurt them; they shall lay hands on the sick, and they shall recover.*

Christ did not ascribe casting out devils to pastors but all that believe. A thing that means a few scare tactics makes the church for the rest of their lives to be dependents on the servant of God. Not by principle but by deceptive means, where even some devils are venerated literally in the church of God before the congregation that they are stronger than them and only the pastor can handle them. It is not true but a limiting factor to make dependents.

Developing A Sure Standard

2 Timothy 2:15-19 KJV *Study to shew thyself approved unto God, a workman that needeth not to be ashamed, rightly dividing the word of truth. But shun profane and vain babblings: for they will increase unto more ungodliness. And their word will eat as doth a canker: of whom is Hymenaeus and Philetus; Who concerning the truth have erred, saying that the resurrection is past already; and overthrow the faith of some. Nevertheless the foundation of God standeth sure, having this seal, The Lord knoweth them that are his. And, Let every one that nameth the name of Christ depart from iniquity.*

Developing a sure standard requites even the noisiest of antagonism. If it is done according to the word by the set standard; then what is there to search out or to weigh in the line of right and wrong. If all is done and set in the weights of truth according to the revealed truth. It would mean a silencing of the sectarian and the destroyer.

When one talks about developing a standard it gets to the question; does it mean we adding in to the word now?

No!

We are simply searching out the word so that we may have a defined standard according to the authority of the word of God and the design of the matter of things as they are happening right now. How did they solve it if they had a hireling then and now and where is the sure balance that we can weigh on what has to be done now; according to the word of God.

The tithe of tithes comes in as that true set standard that was the portion of the Setman since the office was put in place. In it jumping orders and landing in to the another covenant, it should bring with it the same remuneration and effect under the set order not by the former. If there be or was a wage for the hirelings how was it apportioned and how was it collected and paid?

Then through this standard we are able to ascertain a quieting down. That even if it was your kin or distant neighbor you would afford them the same hire for the same service in the eyes of God.

So, without bias you afford it the Setman of God!

The Second And Third Tithes

The Abolished Tithes

The abolished tithes.

When we think of the crucifixion we think only of the conclusion of the Law but there is a lot more that was concluded there upon the cross. The pilgrimages, the sacrifices and some of the tithes that the Law keepers had to endure to fulfill the Law. The crucifixion did not just become the conclusion of the Law. It brings to heart the words of the apostles that they said, that not just themselves but even their fathers failed at fulfilling the Law. So it was fitting to do not inebriate the early church of the gentiles in to the much ado about days and birth rites and circumcision and keeping of holiday and the high Sabbaths and the festivals and the pilgrimages.

One thing that the church often miss is that even the tithe was not just one ten percent of your increase but there were a number of tithes set to satisfy this rites and to maintain even the poor as long as they are of Israel and even the stranger and the fatherless. These tithes were chargeable according to the design of the Law and all fell on the congregants, some to self and some to the needy and some to the priesthood. Yet all in all, every third year Israel had to tithe a clean and clear thirty percent that year. A thing that means of their increase only seventy percent would be their take home.

The conclusion of the Law did curb this. As the church especially the gentile church was never partaker of the three tithe system but only one tithe. Though they of need and necessity had to remember the poor at Jerusalem, it was voluntary and they never had to pay a tithe for the poor that is known not as the second but the third tithe. Meaning there are two other tithes before it being the first tithe to the priesthood, the second tithe to self for pilgrims and holiday festivities and then the tithe for the poor being the third tithe.

Many when they talk about the Law they just see the sacrifices and free will offerings. Yet Israel had to tithe heavily for a guided and fail safe life. They knew they had to fully tithe for their field to yield well year by year. A thing that is said in request of the second tithe not the first; or the festival tithe because they were likely to hold back on this tithe for it was to self. It was not taken to Jerusalem for the Levite or the priest but for them to be joyous and celebrate in the presence of God. In simple terms, God did require feasting and it was financed by the second tithe.

They annually had to go on a holiday by the means of the second tithe.

Deuteronomy 12:5-7 KJV *But unto the place which the LORD your God shall choose out of all your tribes to put his name there, even unto his habitation shall ye seek, and thither thou shalt come: And thither ye shall bring your burnt offerings, and your sacrifices, and your tithes, and heave offerings of your hand, and your vows, and your freewill offerings, and the firstlings of your herds and of your flocks: And there ye shall eat before the LORD your God, and ye shall rejoice in all that ye put your hand unto, ye and your households, wherein the LORD thy God hath blessed thee.*

The second tithe called for feasting and in the presence of God. The second tithe also was often called the tithe of the kraal for most vows and freewill offerings and sacrifices was done amidst this festivities. A thing that means the amenities and firstlings would be abundantly be put on the altar. The thing with this tithe is also one was at liberty to give others to join them in the festivities. A thing that means it covered all Israel with festivities regardless of creed or height or descent.

Here what we simply say is among the things that were abolished with the handwriting of the Law. Two tithes were also announced finished to only live the dues for the servant at the altar of God.

Colossians 2:11-17 KJV *In whom also ye are circumcised with the circumcision made without hands, in putting off the body of the sins of the flesh by the circumcision of Christ: Buried with him in baptism, wherein also ye are risen with him through the faith of the operation of God, who hath raised him from the dead. And you, being dead in your sins and the uncircumcision of your flesh, hath he quickened together with him, having forgiven you all trespasses; Blotting out the handwriting of ordinances that was against us, which was contrary to us, and took it out of the way, nailing it to his cross; And having spoiled principalities and powers, he made a shew of them openly, triumphing over them in it. Let no man therefore judge you in meat, or in drink, or in respect of an holyday, or of the new moon, or of the sabbath days: Which are a shadow of things to come; but the body is of Christ.*

The fulfilling of the Law when Christ said it is finished among the many things did conclude two forms of tithes being:

1. The second tithe- holiday or festival Tithe
2. The third tithe-tithe for the needy

Yes! Puzzling and surprising as it may seem. The needy's tithe was never one with the tithe you pay. It was a totally different and total separately principled tithe: unlike the first and the second tithes that Israel did pay. The tithe for the poor was triennial and was never submitted or was ever meant to be submitted at church. It was put outside the house within the gate for the widow, the fatherless and the stranger to pick and partake.

It was a separate tithe.

The third tithe.

Known as the third tithe, the tithe for the needy was a separate tithe as it was only done once every three years: where as the tithe that is still in effect was done continually year by year along the second tithe which was the festival or holidays festivities tithe which also was not given to the pastor but enjoyed at church by the one who saved it to be happy and festive in the presence of God.

The thing with the third tithe or the tithe for the needy, widow, the fatherless and the stranger was done not by the Levites but within their gates or locality of a city or village. It was not gathered for the Levite there among them but within their jurisdiction of a settlement or city for the poor of that area; if it would be set in a temple it would be just for the needy not that it is for the service of the Levite or the temple. Only they were charged to remember the Levite or the church worker as in other tithes. Not that he will be in control but because it is within the gates and they have to remember the Levite among them.

The first tithe.

So, the notion that pastors should give part of the tithe they receive to the needy and widow is not just absurd but wrong and born of utter ignorance. A thing that means people out of their own bias did desire to place the widow and the needy somewhere whereas they did not know how and where. A thing that usually comes of the common terms of branding the tithe theirs and having a right or say on how it should be spent.

The first tithe is and was always the part that is holy unto God. Meaning thinking that one owns and has a part in it comes out of not knowing all things. It was and will always belong to God. So, thinking tithe belongs to you makes you even think of better things than paying the pastor. Things like buying instruments, building the church or even starting a charitable organization to help the needy or the society or social responsibilities. It is not for that and was never for that and it would never be for that. The first tithe is only and should only be used to remunerate the workers of God's altar, starting first with the vision bearer or the Setman exacting a tithe of tithes through the hand of the pastoral team members. Then the nine percent that remains is not for the church but the livelihood of the family of the church worker and his/her household.

The second tithe.

The other tithe that was abolished by the end of the Law is the festival tithe or the holiday tithe. Israel by default had to annually take three pilgrimages to the city of God three times a year. The third tithe was a form of providence they had or a saving holiday scheme to provide for the pilgrimages and to be festive as they go there. There were a few rites they did at those festivals and all took not from their pockets directly but from their savings plans. Plus the firstling of their kraal and their vows and love offerings and the tithe of the kraal. Though the first fruits were to a due course of being received by the Levitical priesthood for their consumption; the firstlings of the kraal and kraal tithes has differing rites. A sure thing that one would deep self in further to learn and earn more extra knowledge; though covered herein.

So, two tithes were cancelled and one was for the pilgrimage of three holidays a year and another for the poor. So, from hither forth, after this study you will no longer pester or watch with disdain the pastor as the tithe of the poor died with the Law.

So, in keeping no more pilgrimages, it means no more holidays and so no more setting aside savings which happens to be a second tenth of the produce of the field. Meaning they annually had to tithe twenty percent. The first ten percent to God and the second twenty percent to their pleasure. And yet once every three years they had to tithe another ten percent for the needy among them.

Colossians 2:16-18 KJV *Let no man therefore judge you in meat, or in drink, or in respect of an holyday, or of the new moon, or of the sabbath days: Which are a shadow of things to come; but the body is of Christ. Let no man beguile you of your reward in a voluntary humility and worshipping of angels, intruding into those things which he hath not seen, vainly puffed up by his fleshly mind,*

So, the above words of Paul do not just stop the gentile church from observing the Jewish holiday; but also the pilgrimages that were involved and the need to appear before God in Jerusalem three times. So, the second tithe or holiday savings scheme dies. For in this tithe none of it was due to God or His work or servants but to get self filled and family and even for buying strong drink during the days of pilgrimage.

Deuteronomy 16:13-17 KJV *Thou shalt observe the feast of tabernacles seven days, after that thou hast gathered in thy corn and thy wine: And thou shalt rejoice in thy feast, thou, and thy son, and thy daughter, and thy manservant, and thy maidservant, and the Levite, the stranger, and the fatherless, and the widow, that are within thy gates. Seven days shalt thou keep a solemn feast unto the LORD thy God in the place which the LORD shall choose: because the LORD thy God shall bless thee in all thine increase, and in all the works of thine hands, therefore thou shalt surely rejoice. Three times in a year shall all thy males appear before the LORD thy God in the place which he shall choose; in the feast of unleavened bread, and in the feast of weeks, and in the feast of tabernacles: and they shall not appear before the LORD empty: Every man shall give as he is able, according to the blessing of the LORD thy God which he hath given thee.*

The three times they had to appear before God there was a preordained arrangement and they had to go out to Jerusalem and have a feast out of their second tithe and their vows and other offerings. By an ordained Law they did have a second tithe to spend in these pilgrimages three times a year.

So, despite the out cry of the current church; there are two types of tithes that have been abolished in the congregation of God. Both tithes were not dues towards the congregation leadership but open tithes that one was spent on self and one on the needy of Israel, the stranger and the fatherless.

The book of **Deuteronomy** tells you what most would be astonished to hear. Take your tithe to where God has established his name and eat your tithes there; yourself and family and friends. Yet the book of **Numbers** says the tithe is the portion of the Levite. Yet another thing **Deuteronomy** says, lay your tithe at the gate so that the widow, the fatherless and the stranger may partake of them. Another thing that is definitely surprising is that the tithe is holy and should be given unto the Levite among you.

A thing that simply gives you three forms of independent tithes. One to give to the Levite, one to eat and be festive and even buy strong drink out of it in the place that the Lord shall choose for His name to dwell, another to lay within your gates or the gates of your city, which is within your municipality.

Numbers 18:26-32 KJV *Thus speak unto the Levites, and say unto them, When ye take of the children of Israel the tithes which I have given you from them for your inheritance, then ye shall offer up an heave offering of it for the LORD, even a tenth part of the tithe. And this your heave offering shall be reckoned unto you, as though it were the corn of the threshingfloor, and as the fulness of the winepress. Thus ye also shall offer an heave offering unto the LORD of all your tithes, which ye receive of the children of Israel; and ye shall give thereof the LORD'S heave offering to Aaron the priest. Out of all your gifts ye shall offer every heave offering of the LORD, of all the best thereof, even the hallowed part thereof out of it. Therefore thou shalt say unto them, When ye have heaved the best thereof from it, then it shall be counted unto the Levites as the increase of the threshingfloor, and as the increase of the winepress. And ye shall eat it in every place, ye and your households: for it is your reward for your service in the tabernacle of the congregation. And ye shall bear no sin by reason of it, when ye have heaved from it the best of it: neither shall ye pollute the holy things of the children of Israel, lest ye die.*

Leviticus 27:30-33 KJV *And all the tithe of the land, whether of the seed of the land, or of the fruit of the tree, is the LORD'S: it is holy unto the LORD. And if a man will at all redeem ought of his tithes, he shall add thereto the fifth part thereof. And concerning the tithe of the herd, or of the flock, even of whatsoever passeth under the rod, the tenth shall be holy unto the LORD. He shall not search whether it be good or bad, neither shall he change it: and if he change it at all, then both it and the change thereof shall be holy; it shall not be redeemed.*

The above critical statements are soon denied by the book of **Deuteronomy** and so we ought to seat down and break the bones of the word. The ideal being if the tithe belonged to the Levitical priesthood; how then are the children of

Israel also allowed to eat their tithe. And still how are they again allowed to lay it out on their gates for the poor. Here below is a total diametric of the above words about tithes.

Deuteronomy 12:5-7, 11-14, 17-18 KJV *But unto the place which the LORD your God shall choose out of all your tribes to put his name there, even unto his habitation shall ye seek, and thither thou shalt come: And thither ye shall bring your burnt offerings, and your sacrifices, and your tithes, and heave offerings of your hand, and your vows, and your freewill offerings, and the firstlings of your herds and of your flocks: And there ye shall eat before the LORD your God, and ye shall rejoice in all that ye put your hand unto, ye and your households, wherein the LORD thy God hath blessed thee. Then there shall be a place which the LORD your God shall choose to cause his name to dwell there; thither shall ye bring all that I command you; your burnt offerings, and your sacrifices, your tithes, and the heave offering of your hand, and all your choice vows which ye vow unto the LORD: And ye shall rejoice before the LORD your God, ye, and your sons, and your daughters, and your menservants, and your maidservants, and the Levite that is within your gates; forasmuch as he hath no part nor inheritance with you. Take heed to thyself that thou offer not thy burnt offerings in every place that thou seest: But in the place which the LORD shall choose in one of thy tribes, there thou shalt offer thy burnt offerings, and there thou shalt do all that I command thee. Thou mayest not eat within thy gates the tithe of thy corn, or of thy wine, or of thy oil, or the firstlings of thy herds or of thy flock, nor any of thy vows which thou vowest, nor thy freewill offerings, or heave offering of thine hand: But thou must eat them before the LORD thy God in the place which the LORD thy God shall choose, thou, and thy son, and thy daughter, and thy manservant, and thy maidservant, and the Levite that is within thy gates: and thou shalt rejoice before the LORD thy God in all that thou puttest thine hands unto.*

There is a kind of tithe that is introduced to Israel or the congregation in **Deuteronomy 12**, then another in **Deuteronomy 14** along with the formerly introduced tithe in **Deuteronomy 12**. These are the tithes that mostly the church is not aware of: for they are both abolished tithes. So usually when the church talks about the needy and the fatherless partaking of the tithe, they usually forget themselves that there was a tithe that they were supposed to take a tour to the house of God and eat it there. Not give it to the Levites but eat it there and even buy strong drink or any ought and enjoy. The tithe introduce by the twelfth chapter of **Deuteronomy** is simply called the **Second Tithe**.

Deuteronomy 14:22-27 KJV *Thou shalt truly tithe all the increase of thy seed, that the field bringeth forth year by year. And thou shalt eat before the LORD thy God, in the place which he shall choose to place his name there, the tithe of thy corn, of thy wine, and of thine oil, and the firstlings of thy herds and of thy flocks; that thou mayest learn to fear the LORD thy God always. And if the way be too long for thee, so that thou art not able to carry it; or if the place be too far from thee, which the LORD thy God shall choose to set his name there, when the LORD thy God hath blessed thee: Then shalt thou turn it into money, and bind up the money in thine hand, and shalt go unto the place which the LORD thy God shall choose: And thou shalt bestow that money for whatsoever thy soul lusteth after, for oxen, or for sheep, or for wine, or for strong drink,*

or for whatsoever thy soul desireth: and thou shalt eat there before the LORD thy God, and thou shalt rejoice, thou, and thine household, And the Levite that is within thy gates; thou shalt not forsake him; for he hath no part nor inheritance with thee.

Here in the fourteenth chapter yet another tithe is introduced. Here they are told every third year: unlike the tithe they are allowed to go and eat at the temple. Here they are told to lay a tithe on the third year within their gates to allowed the needy among them to partake of it. Which is another tithe; that is commonly known as the **Third Tithe**.

Deuteronomy 14:28-29 KJV *At the end of three years thou shalt bring forth all the tithe of thine increase the same year, and shalt lay it up within thy gates: And the Levite, (because he hath no part nor inheritance with thee,) and the stranger, and the fatherless, and the widow, which are within thy gates, shall come, and shall eat and be satisfied; that the LORD thy God may bless thee in all the work of thine hand which thou doest.*

The second and the third tithe are abolished due to the arrangement of things and change of order. A thing that means the abolishing of holidays meant there is no need for the second tithe. And the whole world instead of the church being the church of God meant the poor would not be manageable as when it was Israel. So, in stead of the third tithe Jesus introduces an new principle. That whoever shall enter by the door shall find pasture; or providence.

John 10:7-10 KJV *Then said Jesus unto them again, Verily, verily, I say unto you, I am the door of the sheep. All that ever came before me are thieves and robbers: but the sheep did not hear them. I am the door: by me if any man enter in, he shall be saved, and shall go in and out, and find pasture. The thief cometh not, but for to steal, and to kill, and to destroy: I am come that they might have life, and that they might have it more abundantly.*

One thing that is often forgotten is that tithe was not initiated by Judaism nor the Jews or Hebrew. As they were even told, whoever they go warring and lay siege they should remember. Before there was a need for man to be redeemed and in the original design of man; the life of man was in the seed. That is Adam was given the seed of the fruit tree to sow back. He was given it way before Judaism multiplied tithe three fold in to the first, second and third. The thing being, even of Abraham we heard he paid a tithe that is way before the Law. Meaning the Law had its version of the tithes but did not start or stop the tithe.

Israel is reminded what was given man in the beginning to sow back; fruit and herbs bearing seed. So that they may saw it back; that is seedtime and harvest. If they endeavored to fulfill the call to fill the earth. They had to sow back in to the kingdom; more seed to expand the garden and the dominion of man. So in **Chronicles** they were reminded where the life of man is.

Deuteronomy 20:19-20 KJV *When thou shalt besiege a city a long time, in making war against it to take it, thou shalt not destroy the trees thereof by forcing an axe against them: for thou mayest eat of them, and thou shalt not cut them down (**for the tree of the field is man's life**) to employ them in the siege: Only the trees which thou knowest that they be not trees for meat, thou shalt destroy and cut them down; and thou shalt build bulwarks against the city that maketh war with thee, until it be subdued.*

As in the beginning they were given the tree of life and many other seed bearing fruit trees and herbs; even in the end they shall be eternally given back the tree with the twelve manner of fruit. So, as it was in the beginning it shall always be. Only the need for redemption takes man to the temporal measure of the cup of blood. Then the eternal rite of the tree of life and the river of life.

Revelation 22:1-5, 14, 17 KJV *And he shewed me a pure river of water of life, clear as crystal, proceeding out of the throne of God and of the Lamb. In the midst of the street of it, and on either side of the river, was there the tree of life, which bare twelve manner of fruits, and yielded her fruit every month: and the leaves of the tree were for the healing of the nations. And there shall be no more curse: but the throne of God and of the Lamb shall be in it; and his servants shall serve him: And they shall see his face; and his name shall be in their foreheads. And there shall be no night there; and they need no candle, neither light of the sun; for the Lord God giveth them light: and they shall reign for ever and ever. Blessed are they that do his commandments, that they may have right to the tree of life, and may enter in through the gates into the city. And the Spirit and the bride say, Come. And let him that heareth say, Come. And let him that is athirst come. And whosoever will, let him take the water of life freely.*

So, as he was given in the beginning it shall be reestablished again here on earth forever. The blessing that points man to the principle of sowing a tithe of all things back is a standard that will hold even beyond the current system of things as he will revert back to the tree of life where he began partaking to keeping yeaning the life of God.

Genesis 1:28-29 KJV *And God blessed them, and God said unto them, Be fruitful, and multiply, and replenish the earth, and subdue it: and have dominion over the fish of the sea, and over the fowl of the air, and over every living thing that moveth upon the earth. And God said, Behold, I have given you every herb bearing seed, which is upon the face of all the earth, and every tree, in the which is the fruit of a tree yielding seed; to you it shall be for meat.*

So, this paternity is passed on to Abraham. Who seemed to have been a constant tither for even when he had refused the gifts of the kings from the slaughter of the four kings. He did of only his spoils of war did give a tithe to the Priest of the Most High God. A thing that tells one he was absorbed by the principle of seedtime and harvest. It was not a random act for he even refused to take of the portion of the profane things of the king of Sodom and his allies. He did not see it fit to be blessed by them, for it would mean they would be a contributing factor to his success a thing that would mean the glorious victories of the Lord are rewarded by them. He rather chose his reward to solely come from God. Making sure not only his tithe but all his substance is still announced holy.

Genesis 14:21-24 KJV *And the king of Sodom said unto Abram, Give me the persons, and take the goods to thyself. And Abram said to the king of Sodom, I have lift up mine hand unto the LORD, the most high God, the possessor of heaven and earth, That I will not take from a thread even to a shoelatchet, and that I will not take any thing that is thine, lest thou shouldest say, I have made Abram rich: Save only that which the young men have eaten, and the portion of the men which went with me, Aner, Eshcol, and Mamre; let them take their portion.*

Upon the spoils of his victory. He refused to take anything from those he rescued. Just the justly warred for stuff and it was it. So of the spoils he did do God the honor.

Hebrews 7:4-17 KJV *Now consider how great this man was, unto whom even the patriarch Abraham gave the tenth of the spoils. And verily they that are of the sons of Levi, who receive the office of the priesthood, have a commandment to take tithes of the people according to the law, that is, of their brethren, though they come out of the loins of Abraham: But he whose descent is not counted from them received tithes of Abraham, and blessed him that had the promises. And without all contradiction the less is blessed of the better. And here men that die receive tithes; but there he receiveth them, of whom it is witnessed that he liveth. And as I may so say, Levi also, who receiveth tithes, payed tithes in Abraham. For he was yet in the loins of his father, when Melchisedec met him. If therefore perfection were by the Levitical priesthood, (for under it the people received the law,) what further need was there that another priest should rise after the order of Melchisedec, and not be called after the order of Aaron? For the priesthood being changed, there is made of necessity a change also of the law. For he of whom these things are spoken pertaineth to another tribe, of which no man gave attendance at the altar. For it is evident that our Lord sprang out of Juda; of which tribe Moses spake nothing concerning priesthood. And it is yet far more evident: for that after the similitude of Melchisedec there ariseth another priest, Who is made, not after the law of a carnal commandment, but after the power of an endless life. For he testifieth, Thou art a priest for ever after the order of Melchisedec.*

The above conclusively tells us, that Christ rises after the similitude of Melchisedek. As Abraham did give a tithe to Melchisedek so arise another worthy in Christ to do take our tithe. For as Melchisedek was to Abraham He is to us; Priest of the Most High instead of Melchisedek. A thing that keeps on the standing Order towards God.

Genesis 14:14-20 KJV *And when Abram heard that his brother was taken captive, he armed his trained servants, born in his own house, three hundred and eighteen, and pursued them unto Dan. And he divided himself against them, he and his servants, by night, and smote them, and pursued them unto Hobah, which is on the left hand of Damascus. And he brought back all the goods, and also brought again his brother Lot, and his goods, and the women also, and the people. And the king of Sodom went out to meet him after his return from the slaughter of Chedorlaomer, and of the kings that were with him, at the valley of Shaveh, which is the king's dale. And Melchizedek king of Salem brought forth bread and wine: and he was the priest of the most high God. And he blessed him, and said, Blessed be Abram of the most high God, possessor of heaven and earth: And blessed be the most high God, which hath delivered thine enemies into thy hand. And he gave him tithes of all.*

Going Extra Curricular

Hello! And please be reminded this study is not what we are supposed to do but extra curricular aimed at self improvement and theological seminary findings of past things in the way. It is to say, the saints of old did keep other things that we do not and this is how they kept them.

So, in reiteration; this is extra curricular!

The extra curricular study of dues ethic talks about the desolate or dysfunctional or concluded part of the dues. Usually when one talks about the part of tithe that is no longer functional; they talk about the Levitical priesthood and the tithe. It is not the pastoral tithe that is no longer functional; it is the third year for the poor and the widow and the annual pilgrimage tithe.

The pastoral tithe stands because the Levitical priesthood was not just concluded but replaced by the system of a new priesthood or set of pastors; meaning there are still men and women dedicated at fully serving God from the altar. A thing that means there is still a need to supplement their efforts with a hire from the congregation of God.

Jeremiah 3:15-16 KJV *And I will give you pastors according to mine heart, which shall feed you with knowledge and understanding. And it shall come to pass, when ye be multiplied and increased in the land, in those days, saith the LORD, they shall say no more, The ark of the covenant of the LORD: neither shall it come to mind: neither shall they remember it; neither shall they visit it; neither shall that be done any more.*

There was not an abolishing or finishing of the priesthood in heaven which the pastoral and priesthood on earth is under. Rather the title of the Highpriest in heaven was translated to the new pastors on earth being a new priesthood according to the gifting of the Son. Melchisedek's priesthood moved for the Jesus Christ's priesthood. Meaning who was priest over the Levites had to come down and die so that He may transfer the priesthood to all humanity from the house of Aaron.

Hebrews 5:1-14 KJV *For every high priest taken from among men is ordained for men in things pertaining to God, that he may offer both gifts and sacrifices for sins: Who can have compassion on the ignorant, and on them that are out of the way; for that he himself also is compassed with infirmity. And by reason hereof he ought, as for the people, so also for himself, to offer for sins. And no man taketh this honour unto himself, but he that is called of God, as was Aaron. So also Christ glorified not himself to be made an high priest; but he that said unto him, Thou art my Son, to day have I begotten thee. As he saith also in another place, Thou art a priest for ever after the order of Melchisedec. Who in the days of his flesh,* *when he had offered up prayers and supplications with strong crying and tears unto him that was able to save him from death, and was heard in that he feared; Though he were a Son, yet learned he obedience by the things which he suffered; And being made perfect, he became the author of eternal salvation unto all them that obey him; Called of God an high priest after the order of Melchisedec. Of whom we have many things to say, and hard to be uttered, seeing ye are dull of hearing. For when for the time ye ought to be teachers, ye have need that one teach you again which be the first principles of the oracles of God; and are become such as have need of milk, and not of strong meat. For every one that useth milk is unskilful in the word of righteousness: for he is a babe. But strong meat belongeth to them that are of full age, even those who by reason of use have their senses exercised to discern both good and evil.*

Extra studies like this one are often termed the meat of the theologian but at times it is important to indulge to know how things did transverse and reshape themselves on to a new faith; Christianity. As most cross roads are not to be missed and are returned to even what went athwart in principle and order has optimal meaning when well articulated and understood. It becomes a guide to the favor grace has earned us under the current dispensation in comparison to those who did walk the walk of faith before us.

The office of the priest or the pastor was not abandoned but it was reformed. As the priesthood is no longer by linage as even the Highpriest is a break away from the Aaron priesthood and the Mosaic Accord. He is from a separate tribe and even the priests of the better covenant are not chosen by being part of a family but they are normally chosen by Him. A thing that means He is still in the office of hiring servants for His field.

Ephesians 4:8-15 KJV *Wherefore he saith, When he ascended up on high, he led captivity captive, and gave gifts unto men. (Now that he ascended, what is it but that he also descended first into the lower parts of the earth? He that descended is the same also that ascended up far above all heavens, that he might fill all things.) And he gave some, apostles; and some, prophets; and some, evangelists; and some, pastors and teachers; For the perfecting of the saints, for the work of the ministry, for the edifying of the body of Christ: Till we all come in the unity of the faith, and of the knowledge of the Son of God, unto a perfect man, unto the measure of the stature of the fulness of Christ: That we henceforth be no more children, tossed to and fro, and carried about with every wind of doctrine, by the sleight of men, and cunning craftiness, whereby they lie in wait to deceive; But speaking the truth in love, may grow up into him in all things, which is the head, even Christ:*

Christ when was lifted raised a new priesthood among men. He did give them as a gift to His church meaning as the Levitical priesthood was given a gift to the congregation Israel even now the church has been given the man to stand at the altar of God for their sakes; so that they may know Him and be perfected in to Him in all things. This change of **Covenant** and **Order** means things are no longer as they were; but a new church leadership was gazette the whole world as the expansion and field of work. The workers were even given a new change of Order. As Christ told them face to face if they delayed the more and more others would be added in to the field until it is time to conclude day time or the work of God.

John 11:7-10 KJV *Then after that saith he to his disciples, Let us go into Judaea again. His disciples say unto him, Master, the Jews of late sought to stone thee; and goest thou thither again? Jesus answered, Are there not twelve hours in the day? If any man walk in the day, he stumbleth not, because he seeth the light of this world. But if a man walk in the night, he stumbleth, because there is no light in him.*

It is the day or the time of enlightenment or understanding that enables us to do God's work not by the measure of limit of darkness but light in us and for us. That is why Christ did say to His disciples it is day. Like a candle lit; He knew no one could or would deny it is the whole truth they can be enlightened the easy way or the hard way. So, even these hirelings that He did put in to the field first being the apostles He said to them. If they tarry and waste time. He would even the more and more get more workers until the end of day; a thing that means it is not by tribe and linage: but the key thing is He is still getting workers for a certain hire. He also put the elaboration that it shall not be increased or decreased; but be the same hire; the same tenth or the penny for all.

A thing that means the tithe as was will be and shall always be the hire of the shepherd or the reaper or worker in the field until the end of time or the system of things as we know them. As a standing principle or perpetual Principle, the dues ethic will gain or lose some shape along the way according to His design and desire. A thing that means as covenant and orders change the method and the design changes. One sure thing being from Adam to Israel God was served in agrarian societies; but the modern church is a thriving concrete jungle church meaning the earnings and the tithe are things of the enterprising society.

It does not begin now. For even then when Caesar came in with money they came to try Christ on that lot. If they should being an agrarian society pay penny dues to Caesar and Christ did answer in a solid way. The dynamics did change for upon the three tithes they had to pay tribute to Caesar; an additional forth tithe one would say. Yet even in our dynamic society one would ask of taxes payable and tithe if it should come before or after taxes. Still one has to say it like Christ said it; give the state what belongs to the state and give God what belongs to God.

One would say it was an easier thing to say then. For the tithes were agrarian and Caesar's portion monetary and now both the government and God receive monetary dues.

Matthew 22:15-21 KJV *Then went the Pharisees, and took counsel how they might entangle him in his talk. And they sent out unto him their disciples with the Herodians, saying, Master, we know that thou art true, and teachest the way of God in truth, neither carest thou for any man: for thou regardest not the person of men. Tell us therefore, What thinkest* thou? Is it lawful to give tribute unto Caesar, or not?But Jesus perceived their wickedness, and said, Why tempt ye me, ye hypocrites? Shew me the tribute money. And they brought unto him a penny. And he saith unto them, Whose is this image and superscription? They say unto him, Caesar's. Then saith he unto them, Render therefore unto Caesar the things which are Caesar's; and unto God the things that are God's.*

The above was a cross road that proved opportune even to the pharisees for they used it to ensnare Christ. Yet in reality it was a timely question then. The ideal being it proved a doubt towards the defense and the plan of God for them.

How does God enslave them though they are expected to be loyal to Him?

It was not eminent but it was happening for they had to co-rule with Rome in all things. Yet Rome was above them in all things. Even playing slave master over them. It was a passing phase of the three tithes system where they had to pay a forth tithe or tax or tribute to their conqueror and still pay their dues to God. This is the same season that even Christ came to send His own in the field for a hire. One would say the entry of Caesar proved plausible as even Paul used it to escape beatings and surmising by the Jews.

Acts 22:24-30 KJV *The chief captain commanded him to be brought into the castle, and bade that he should be examined by scourging; that he might know wherefore they cried so against him. And as they bound him with thongs, Paul said unto the centurion that stood by, Is it lawful for you to scourge a man that is a Roman, and uncondemned? When the centurion heard that, he went and told the chief captain, saying, Take heed what thou doest: for this man is a Roman. Then the chief captain came, and said unto him, Tell me, art thou a Roman? He said, Yea. And the chief captain answered, With a great sum obtained I this freedom. And Paul said, But I was free born. Then straightway they departed from him which should have examined him: and the chief captain also was afraid, after he knew that he was a Roman, and because he had bound him. On the morrow, because he would have known the certainty wherefore he was accused of the Jews, he loosed him from his bands, and commanded the chief priests and all their council to appear, and brought Paul down, and set him before them.*

So, there in the season of the crossroads of the Roman and The Jew the kingdom of part clay and part iron; He came in as that stone not cut by hand to be the kingdom that shall never stop growing until it swallows the earth. He comes wrapped in the prophecy of **Daniel** not on His own; but introducing a priesthood. Named according to His will apostle, prophets, pastors, evangelists and teachers. And say to them being the chosen, many shall be called. Yet between the chosen and the called the hire shall be same; a penny a day. Meaning they the apostles as the others that shall be called shall all be liable to a price of a hireling through their generations. That is what and how Christ talks about the principle of dues in the diametric change of order from Melchisedek to Christ. He did instate a wage for the apostle, for the prophet, for the evangelist for the pastor and for the teacher here. All in parable so the simple could not discern. And when asked, this is where you tell them; before He gave the church to Peter as promised He established that they shall be a hire that is the same for all; being the usual pay; a tithe of all things. He does not add the more workers; but they are all duly paid; the same pay of a hireling a day.

Matthew 20:2-16 KJV *And when he had agreed with the labourers for a penny a day, he sent them into his vineyard. And he went out about the third hour, and saw others standing idle in the marketplace, And said unto them; Go ye also into the vineyard, and whatsoever is right I will give you. And they went their way. Again he went out about the sixth and ninth hour, and did likewise. And about the eleventh hour he went out, and found others standing idle, and saith unto them, Why stand ye here all the day idle? They say unto him, Because no man hath hired us. He saith unto them, Go ye also into the vineyard; and whatsoever is right, that shall ye receive. So when even was come, the lord of the vineyard saith unto his steward, Call the labourers, and give them their hire, beginning from the last unto the first. And when they came that were hired about the eleventh hour, they received every man a penny. But when the first came, they supposed that they should have received more; and they likewise received every man a penny. And when they had received it, they murmured against the goodman of the house, Saying, These last have wrought but one hour, and thou hast made them equal unto us, which have borne the burden and heat of the day. But he answered one of them, and said, Friend, I do thee no wrong: didst not thou agree with me for a penny? Take that thine is, and go thy way: I will give unto this last, even as unto thee. Is it not lawful for me to do what I will with mine own? Is thine eye evil, because I am good? So the last shall be first, and the first last: for many be called, but few chosen.*

The thing with the new hire is that it comes with a new commission. Instead of just taking care of a people. They are set and sent to the whole world and all peoples. And as He said it; He chose only the twelve but He of His own addition knew he would add men like Stephen, Paul, Phillip and Barnabas to go in to the field among the first apostles. Of the chosen twelve He knew; shall rise more and even be much more than the first apostles. For the said promise and for the said hire and pay.

Matthew 20:16 KJV *So the last shall be first, and the first last: for many be called, but few chosen.*

Matthew 19:27-30 KJV *Then answered Peter and said unto him, Behold, we have forsaken all, and followed thee; what shall we have therefore? And Jesus said unto them, Verily I say unto you, That ye which have followed me, in the regeneration when the Son of man shall sit in the throne of his glory, ye also shall sit upon twelve thrones, judging the twelve tribes of Israel. And every one that hath forsaken houses, or brethren, or sisters, or father, or mother, or wife, or children, or lands, for my name's sake, shall receive an hundredfold, and shall inherit everlasting life. But many that are first shall be last; and the last shall be first.*

Meaning as the need rises and the increase is made; there is a need for more to be sent in to the field but by default; so it can not be just a certain group of people but peoples. People of many tongues as seen by Isaiah though it provokes Israel to jealousy.

Isaiah 28:7-29 KJV *But they also have erred through wine, and through strong drink are out of the way; the priest and the prophet have erred through strong drink, they are swallowed up of wine, they are out of the way through strong drink; they err in vision, they stumble in judgment. For all tables are full of vomit and filthiness, so that there is no place clean. Whom shall he teach knowledge? And whom shall he make to understand doctrine? Them that are weaned from the milk, and drawn from the breasts. For precept must be upon precept, precept upon precept; line upon line, line upon line; here a little, and there a little: For with stammering lips and another tongue will he speak to this people. To whom he said, This is the rest wherewith ye may cause the weary to rest; and this is the refreshing: yet they would not hear. But the word of the LORD was unto them precept upon precept, precept upon precept; line upon line, line upon line; here a little, and there a little; that they might go, and fall backward, and be broken, and snared, and taken. Wherefore hear the word of the LORD, ye scornful men, that rule this people which is in Jerusalem. Because ye have said, We have made a covenant with death, and with hell are we at agreement; when the overflowing scourge shall pass through, it shall not come unto us: for we have made lies our refuge, and under falsehood have we hid ourselves: Therefore thus saith the Lord GOD, Behold, I lay in Zion for a foundation a stone, a tried stone, a precious corner stone, a sure foundation: he that believeth shall not make haste. Judgment also will I lay to the line, and righteousness to the plummet: and the hail shall sweep away the refuge of lies, and the waters shall overflow the hiding place. And your covenant with death shall be disannulled, and your agreement with hell shall not stand; when the overflowing scourge shall pass through, then ye shall be trodden down by it. From the time that it goeth forth it shall take you: for morning by morning shall it pass over, by day and by night: and it shall be a vexation only to understand the report. For the bed is shorter than that a man can stretch himself on it: and the covering narrower than that he can wrap himself in it. For the LORD shall rise up as in mount Perazim, he shall be wroth as in the valley of Gibeon, that he may do his work, his strange work; and bring to pass his act, his strange act. Now therefore be ye not mockers, lest your bands be made strong: for I have heard from the Lord GOD of hosts a consumption, even determined upon the whole earth. Give ye ear, and hear my voice; hearken, and hear my speech. Doth the plowman plow all day to sow? Doth he open and break the clods of his ground? When he hath made plain the face thereof, doth he not cast abroad the fitches, and scatter the cummin, and cast in the principal wheat and the appointed barley and the rie in their place? For his God doth instruct him to discretion, and doth teach him. For the fitches are not threshed with a threshing instrument, neither is a cart wheel turned about upon the cummin; but the fitches are beaten out with a staff, and the cummin with a rod. Bread corn is bruised; because he will not ever be threshing it, nor break it with the wheel of his cart, nor bruise it with his horsemen. This also cometh forth from the LORD of hosts, which is wonderful in counsel, and excellent in working.*

So as He promised above from the corner stone He did send off the apostles to the whole world. Adding new sheep that were not of the former kraal. This shift of things mean it is not longer only about Israel but humanity which it is the desire of God that it all be saved. A thing that means men like Timothy who would have been reduced to being called Samaritan because of being born between a Jew and a foreigner was nullified; and he stood aptly to do the evangelistic work of God according to the call.

1 Timothy 2:1-6 KJV *I exhort therefore, that, first of all, supplications, prayers, intercessions, and giving of thanks, be made for all men; For kings, and for all that are in authority; that we may lead a quiet and peaceable life in all godliness and honesty. For this is good and acceptable in the sight of God our Saviour; Who will have all men to be saved, and to come unto the knowledge of the truth. For there is one God, and one mediator between God and men, the man Christ Jesus; Who gave himself a ransom for all, to be testified in due time.*

The preamble of the tithes paid by Israel clears to just one under the grace for all. As Christ do send them to seek the lost of the whole world. Taking the audacity from Jewry who were formerly the only congregation of God; to the whole world who had been strangers to the common wealth of God. This shift of covenant bring a shift in order. The church leader is no longer just Levi but men chosen and men called. A thing that later adds the empty office by putting in two other offices by the need of service in the gentile church; bishops and deacons.

Matthew 28:18-20 KJV *And Jesus came and spake unto them, saying, All power is given unto me in heaven and in earth. Go ye therefore, and teach all nations, baptizing them in the name of the Father, and of the Son, and of the Holy Ghost: Teaching them to observe all things whatsoever I have commanded you: and, lo, I am with you always, even unto the end of the world. Amen.*

In simple terms; from the day of sending for by the great commission, God no longer saw His congregation as a people but all peoples. Then in seeing all peoples as His peoples; it meant the whole world would be liable to partaking on the tithe of the needy as did Israel. A thing that means it would no longer be functional. As laying the tithe for the needy outside the gate or leaving it outside would mean a world scramble and mostly to the wrong people.

It had to be for the needy among the congregation and it was not supposed to be brought to church or temple. A thing that meant it was supposed to not be given specifically to any directly. But left out for any and all the needy of Israel to pick and help self. One other thing that most people do not know is that; the tithe for the needy was not part of the first ten percent nor part of the second ten percent; which is the pilgrimage tithe or festival tithe or second tithe.

Meaning of you inquire about the ration of he poor, it is not your pastor who is robbing the poor but you. The tithe for the poor like gleaning was a third ten percent that Israel had to offer and by constraint fully for the increase of the field.

It was not deducted from the first ten percent but it was another ten percent dedicated to the poor every three years. In simple terms to sort a beginning we should go back to picking the way of tithing in the congregation of Israel to be able to build a solid and desired understanding for the reader.

The ideal is to look in to the usual questions being the following by breaking the tithes in to independent headings and explaining each independently. The usual undercover question of the church is:

Where is the tithe part of the poor?

Giving birth to minor questions like:

Are we failing God by not providing for the poor?

Do the servants of God now go beyond their portion of call and eat all tithe and leave out the widow, the fatherless and the poor?

So, to answer that, here below we do go into the abolished tithes to see which was for the poor by separating the other two tithes from the hire of the pastor. A thing that will hither forth wash clean many's conscience as the questions are often sparked by a lack of understanding clearly how the poor were provided for and what salvation brought to the new congregation.

This extra curricular study is meant to further separate the three tithes so that we may be at liberty by understanding the their standing order and what they were utilized to do. A thing that means we are going to dig further out of our gazette study so that we may know what caused the change of heart and design of tithes as they were. One candid thing being out of the three tithes that Israel paid only one is left and it has a course and a purpose to fulfill in the church of God.

Then one would ask; was there a real need to structure it as it is?

There was a dire need as the things they served proved desolate and they would be called for in an uncircumspect manner making them irrelevant. In simple terms, they were unhinging the current principles of Grace as we no longer live by the Law but by principle under Grace. The simple and perfect answer would be. Under the Law Christ did deliberately say we will always have the poor among us. Yet when He talks about those who shall be saved He says whoever will enter by Him will be saved, go in and out and find pasture. Meaning poverty has been rendered desolate and so the need for allocating for it would speak against the principle of salvation.

John 10:9-11 KJV *I am the door: by me if any man enter in, he shall be saved, and shall go in and out, and find pasture. The thief cometh not, but for to steal, and to kill, and to destroy: I am come that they might have life, and that they might have it more abundantly. I am the good shepherd: the good shepherd giveth his life for the sheep.*

The thief in the above scripture refers to the whole era of Aaron or Levitical priesthood. They did come holding the shadow of things as if they were true even though the Law could not make any fit or saved for it did not even have the strength to forgive sins. They literally had to sell their sins to the priest with goat all year long. Meaning as he partook of the goat he did not lead them to forgiveness but bore the sin in his flesh until he laid the sin on the Azazel to go without the camp with it. A thing meaning standing there confessing their sins was a worthless as any who stayed at home without effort: except when they brought a goat to sell away their sins.

Leviticus 16:5, 7-31 KJV *And he shall take of the congregation of the children of Israel two kids of the goats for a sin offering, and one ram for a burnt offering. And he shall take the two goats, and present them before the LORD at the door of the tabernacle of the congregation. And Aaron shall cast lots upon the two goats; one lot for the LORD, and the other lot for the scapegoat. And Aaron shall bring the goat upon which the LORD'S lot fell, and offer him for a sin offering. But the goat, on which the lot fell to be the scapegoat, shall be presented alive before the LORD, to make an atonement with him, and to let him go for a scapegoat into the wilderness. And Aaron shall bring the bullock of the sin offering, which is for himself, and shall make an atonement for himself, and for his house, and shall kill the bullock of the sin offering which is for himself: And he shall take a censer full of burning coals of fire from off the altar before the LORD, and his hands full of sweet incense beaten small, and bring it within the vail: And he shall put the incense upon the fire before the LORD, that the cloud of the incense may cover the mercy seat that is upon the testimony, that he die not: And he shall take of the blood of the bullock, and sprinkle it with his finger upon the mercy seat eastward; and before the mercy seat shall he sprinkle of the blood with his finger seven times. Then shall he kill the goat of the sin offering, that is for the people, and bring his blood within the vail, and do with that blood as he did with the blood of the bullock, and sprinkle it upon the mercy seat, and before the mercy seat: And he shall make an atonement for the holy place, because of the uncleanness of the children of Israel, and because of their transgressions in all their sins: and so shall he do for the tabernacle of the congregation, that remaineth among them in the midst of their uncleanness. And there shall be no man in the tabernacle of the congregation when he goeth in to make an atonement in the holy place, until he come out, and have made an atonement for himself, and for his household, and for all the congregation of Israel. And he shall go out unto the altar that is before the LORD, and make an atonement for it; and shall take of the blood of the bullock, and of the blood of the goat, and put it upon the horns of the altar round about. And he shall sprinkle of the blood upon it with his finger seven times, and cleanse it, and hallow it from the uncleanness of the children of Israel. And when he hath made an end of reconciling the holy place, and the tabernacle of the congregation, and* *the altar, he shall bring the live goat: And Aaron shall lay both his hands upon the head of the live goat, and confess over him all the iniquities of the children of Israel, and all their transgressions in all their sins, putting them upon the head of the goat, and shall send him away by the hand of a fit man into the wilderness: And the goat shall bear upon him all their iniquities unto a land not inhabited: and he shall let go the goat in the wilderness. And Aaron shall come into the tabernacle of the congregation, and shall put off the linen garments, which he put on when he went into the holy place, and shall leave them there: And he shall wash his flesh with water in the holy place, and put on his garments, and come forth, and offer his burnt offering, and the burnt offering of the people, and make an atonement for himself, and for the people. And the fat of the sin offering shall he burn upon the altar. And he that let go the goat for the scapegoat shall wash his clothes, and bathe his flesh in water, and afterward come into the camp. And the bullock for the sin offering, and the goat for the sin offering, whose blood was brought in to make atonement in the holy place, shall one carry forth without the camp; and they shall burn in the fire their skins, and their flesh, and their dung. And he that burneth them shall wash his clothes, and bathe his flesh in water, and afterward he shall come into the camp. And this shall be a statute for ever unto you: that in the seventh month, on the tenth day of the month, ye shall afflict your souls, and do no work at all, whether it be one of your own country, or a stranger that sojourneth among you: For on that day shall the priest make an atonement for you, to cleanse you, that ye may be clean from all your sins before the LORD. It shall be a sabbath of rest unto you, and ye shall afflict your souls, by a statute for ever.*

So, with that principle Christ does deal away with the need to raise a tithe for the needy. Meaning if we do things right, we will be able to prosper in our own lives. Meaning salvation does not just bring in the life but also the peace and providence. As long as we go looking for that pasture or providence and we know Him we are bound to come full. As a principle and not just to some.

What is it that you have prepared and trained for?

You go after it; when you are fully set in Christ you are bringing it home; as a principle. Not the one who hands have been laid upon or has out done any; but the one who knows Him. This simple example is meant to solidify the need to know. And we would only be able to know if we compare the past with the present and the future. Meaning we are purposely going extra curricular to dig deeper for the meaning of the current system of things as they are given to us.

The Three Tithes That Were Paid By Israel

The three tithes.

The three tithes on their own mean the term of the Law did bring in a few changes to tithing and at the end of the Law the adjustment was reversed to set the standard to where it was before. Back to one tithe being the tithe due to the priest of God. Though an adjustment not to the origination of seedtime and harvest. It did send us back at the issue during the times of the patriarchs. They did voluntarily do give a tenth of all things back to God by design and as a way of procuring continuance and yield in their endeavors.

A single ten percent.

It was a single ten percent as promised by Jacob and was given by Abraham that was the order of tithing in their days. A thing that means according to the needs and God's desire to satiate Israel in their pilgrimages and in their Law enforced life; He had to govern further the way of tithing. A thing that does not just affect the dues but also how they do offerings.

Genesis 28:20-22 KJV *And Jacob vowed a vow, saying, If God will be with me, and will keep me in this way that I go, and will give me bread to eat, and raiment to put on, So that I come again to my father's house in peace; then shall the LORD be my God: And this stone, which I have set for a pillar, shall be God's house: and of all that thou shalt give me I will surely give the tenth unto thee.*

Jacob's promise was not complicated to God. God gives him his requests, he returns safe, he would first give his tithe, then he did a schedule of dedication for his generations that the house of God would be built in Bethel. A thing that means his tithing would not just engage him but also his generations as they were tied to his oath that the house of God will be built there. A thing that happens way over four hundred years later by the building of the temple by King Solomon in the place of King David. By the schedule of dedication it had to be built in Bethel and it was later named the city of David or the city of the king.

2 Chronicles 5:1-14 KJV *Thus all the work that Solomon made for the house of the LORD was finished: and Solomon brought in all the things that David his father had dedicated; and the silver, and the gold, and all the instruments, put he among the treasures of the house of God. Then Solomon assembled the elders of Israel, and all the heads of the tribes, the chief of the fathers of the children of Israel, unto Jerusalem, to bring up the ark of the covenant of the LORD out of the city of David, which is Zion. Wherefore all the men of Israel assembled themselves unto the king in the feast which was in the* *seventh month. And all the elders of Israel came; and the Levites took up the ark. And they brought up the ark, and the tabernacle of the congregation, and all the holy vessels that were in the tabernacle, these did the priests and the Levites bring up. Also king Solomon, and all the congregation of Israel that were assembled unto him before the ark, sacrificed sheep and oxen, which could not be told nor numbered for multitude. And the priests brought in the ark of the covenant of the LORD unto his place, to the oracle of the house, into the most holy place, even under the wings of the cherubims: For the cherubims spread forth their wings over the place of the ark, and the cherubims covered the ark and the staves thereof above. And they drew out the staves of the ark, that the ends of the staves were seen from the ark before the oracle; but they were not seen without. And there it is unto this day. There was nothing in the ark save the two tables which Moses put therein at Horeb, when the LORD made a covenant with the children of Israel, when they came out of Egypt. And it came to pass, when the priests were come out of the holy place: (for all the priests that were present were sanctified, and did not then wait by course: Also the Levites which were the singers, all of them of Asaph, of Heman, of Jeduthun, with their sons and their brethren, being arrayed in white linen, having cymbals and psalteries and harps, stood at the east end of the altar, and with them an hundred and twenty priests sounding with trumpets:) It came even to pass, as the trumpeters and singers were as one, to make one sound to be heard in praising and thanking the LORD; and when they lifted up their voice with the trumpets and cymbals and instruments of musick, and praised the LORD, saying, For he is good; for his mercy endureth for ever: that then the house was filled with a cloud, even the house of the LORD; So that the priests could not stand to minister by reason of the cloud: for the glory of the LORD had filled the house of God.*

There was a deliberate shift in tithing that was brought in by the introduction of Judaism. Meaning before Judaism there was a tithing system that was just a single ten percent.

The current system of tithing is not a progression but a reverting back to way that was before the Law. Though not the original or the system of the origination of seedtime and harvest. Where man was given the seed of the fruit and the herb to sow back in to the soil to cater for the expansion of humanity. Though simplistically tithe still does the same. By preserving the seed of God in a man who is able to only dedicate self to just sowing in to human spirits the ideals of the things of God. In the begin sin was set aside and interrupting.

Romans 5:12-21 (KJV) Wherefore, as by one man sin entered into the world, and death by sin; and so death passed upon all men, for that all have sinned:

(For until the law sin was in the world: but sin is not imputed when there is no law.

Nevertheless death reigned from Adam to Moses, even over them that had not sinned after the similitude of Adam's transgression, who is the figure of him that was to come.

But not as the offence, so also is the free gift. For if through the offence of one many be dead, much more the grace of God, and the gift by grace, which is by one man, Jesus Christ, hath abounded unto many.

And not as it was by one that sinned, so is the gift: for the judgment was by one to condemnation, but the free gift is of many offences unto justification.

For if by one man's offence death reigned by one; much more they which receive abundance of grace and of the gift of righteousness shall reign in life by one, Jesus Christ.)

Therefore as by the offence of one judgment came upon all men to condemnation; even so by the righteousness of one the free gift came upon all men unto justification of life.

For as by one man's disobedience many were made sinners, so by the obedience of one shall many be made righteous. Moreover the law entered, that the offence might abound. But where sin abounded, grace did much more abound:

That as sin hath reigned unto death, even so might grace reign through righteousness unto eternal life by Jesus Christ our Lord.

So, originally the tithe or seed was given man to just show back in a land and place watering self and free of any thorns and thistles. Now we are sowing by for in to world full of weed and thorns and many other noises. So, the seed of life is even sown in to the blood of Jesus. The current tithe goes with current system where we are watching and growing the church among thorns and thistles and there is a need for a man to watch the altar of God lest it b profaned. Men set at only doing that are raised for that purpose; by the empty office or the call of God. It cannot just grow on its own as before the fall. Or many would deceivers would derail the whole crop of God to destruction.

2 John 1:7-11 KJV *For many deceivers are entered into the world, who confess not that Jesus Christ is come in the flesh. This is a deceiver and an antichrist. Look to yourselves, that we lose not those things which we have wrought, but that we receive a full reward. Whosoever transgresseth, and abideth not in the doctrine of Christ, hath not God. He that abideth in the doctrine of Christ, he hath both the Father and the Son. If there come any unto you, and bring not this doctrine, receive him not into your house, neither bid him God speed: For he that biddeth him God speed is partaker of his evil deeds.*

Matthew 7:15-27 KJV *Beware of false prophets, which come to you in sheep's clothing, but inwardly they are ravening wolves. Ye shall know them by their fruits. Do men gather grapes of thorns, or figs of thistles? Even so every good tree bringeth forth good fruit; but a corrupt tree bringeth forth evil fruit. A good tree cannot bring forth evil fruit, neither can a corrupt tree bring forth good fruit. Every tree that bringeth not forth good fruit is hewn down, and cast into the fire. Wherefore by their fruits ye shall know them. Not every one that saith unto me, Lord, Lord, shall enter into the kingdom of heaven; but he that doeth the will of my Father which is in heaven. Many will say to me in that day, Lord, Lord, have we not prophesied in thy name? and in thy name have cast out devils? and in thy name done many wonderful works? And then will I profess unto them, I never knew you: depart from me, ye that work iniquity. Therefore whosoever heareth these sayings of mine, and doeth them, I will liken him unto a wise man, which built his house upon a rock: And the rain descended, and the floods came, and the winds blew, and beat upon that house; and it fell not: for it was founded upon a rock. And every one that heareth these sayings of mine, and doeth them not, shall be likened unto a foolish man, which built his house upon the sand: And the rain descended, and the floods came, and the winds blew, and beat upon that house; and it fell: and great was the fall of it.*

Acts 20:29-38 KJV *For I know this, that after my departing shall grievous wolves enter in among you, not sparing the flock. Also of your own selves shall men arise, speaking perverse things, to draw away disciples after them. Therefore watch, and remember, that by the space of three years I ceased not to warn every one night and day with tears. And now, brethren, I commend you to God, and to the word of his grace, which is able to build you up, and to give you an inheritance among all* *them which are sanctified. I have coveted no man's silver, or gold, or apparel. Yea, ye yourselves know, that these hands have ministered unto my necessities, and to them that were with me. I have shewed you all things, how that so labouring ye ought to support the weak, and to remember the words of the Lord Jesus, how he said, It is more blessed to give than to receive. And when he had thus spoken, he kneeled down, and prayed with them all. And they all wept sore, and fell on Paul's neck, and kissed him, Sorrowing most of all for the words which he spake, that they should see his face no more. And they accompanied him unto the ship.*

As long as a man has to leave his way of life and dedicate self to the office of call; they shall be there for a hire. It is so because original there was no need for an altar or to raise a defense against evil. There all humanity was set and ordained and blessed be fruitful and multiply but because of rain war men by design and change of order are now forced to leave their all in order to serve the church of God. Wolves as also do offences cannot by any means not come as foretold by Christ and even the apostles.

They are due and there has to be a system in place to guard them. Before the need to curb offences and wolves he seed on its pure form was enough to sustain and develop man in to the much needed increase. Yet the introduction sin means we can no longer just depend on the seed to grow silently on it s own. The enemy keeps sowing his own seed. A thing that means we need watchmen to build and to curb and design the growth and service of the seed or field until the harvest is mature. To work the field until it be ripe for the harvest. Yet that works receive pay; that sows and that harvest both get wages.

John 4:34-38 KJV *Jesus saith unto them, My meat is to do the will of him that sent me, and to finish his work. Say not ye, There are yet four months, and then cometh harvest? behold, I say unto you, Lift up your eyes, and look on the fields; for they are white already to harvest. And he that reapeth receiveth wages, and gathereth fruit unto life eternal: that both he that soweth and he that reapeth may rejoice together. And herein is that saying true, One soweth, and another reapeth. I sent you to reap that whereon ye bestowed no labour: other men laboured, and ye are entered into their labours.*

The above words say they receive wages. As Paul did say if the churches of Macedonia and Achaia. They are that sow and reap and they are work men for God. A thing that means he will have the means and a way to sustain them. The battle is not theirs but the Lord's and they are not harvesting for themselves but for he silos of God.

1 Corinthians 9:7-14 KJV *Who goeth a warfare any time at his own charges? Who planteth a vineyard, and eateth not of the fruit thereof? Or who feedeth a flock, and eateth not of the milk of the flock? Say I these things as a man? Or saith not the law the same also? For it is written in the law of Moses, Thou shalt not muzzle the mouth of the ox that treadeth out the corn. Doth God take care for oxen? Or saith he it altogether for our sakes? For our sakes, no doubt, this is written: that he that ploweth should plow in hope; and that he that thresheth in hope should be partaker of his hope. If we have sown unto* *you spiritual things, is it a great thing if we shall reap your carnal things? If others be partakers of this power over you, are not we rather? Nevertheless we have not used this power; but suffer all things, lest we should hinder the gospel of Christ. Do ye not know that they which minister about holy things live of the things of the temple? And they which wait at the altar are partakers with the altar? Even so hath the Lord ordained that they which preach the gospel should live of the gospel.*

2 Timothy 2:3-7 KJV *Thou therefore endure hardness, as a good soldier of Jesus Christ. No man that warreth entangleth himself with the affairs of this life; that he may please him who hath chosen him to be a soldier. And if a man also strive for masteries, yet is he not crowned, except he strive lawfully. The husbandman that laboureth must be first partaker of the fruits. Consider what I say; and the Lord give thee understanding in all things.*

Before this things were set and give a sure form. They had to go through the trying and testing of the shadow of things. For which along came the Law and did introduce the two other tithes being the second and the third tithe. A thing that did typify the name from tithe to tithes. Here below are the three told apart:

The First Tithe

The standing tithe.

Yes!, the standing tithe: of the three tithes that were paid by Israel one remains and is currently the only one in place and effect. The first tithe.
    The first tithe or the portion that is holy unto God is the only remaining form of tithing that is set aside as the hire of the servant of God.

This tithe was paid by Israel as a lump some ten percent. Then within the hands of the Levites it was sundered in to a two part tithe system to the Levite and the Setman or the Highpriest. A tenth was thus taken first from it to be the pay for the Highpriest then the rest went to the Levites.

The ideal being, the Setman or the Highpriest was overseer of all Israel as the church overseer still is to the whole church of God; all Israel came to him three times any given year to make mention before God. The watchman at the branch level and those holding the arm's reach of the individual branches together without him and his lot were and are entitled to nine percent of the ten percent the church pays. Then only one percent of the tithe is passed on to the Setman as he is part of all the churches and must be a partaker and servant to all churches. All the burdens and travels and the works for all the branches and headquarters are provided for by this portion from all branches. That is why Paul was not receiving a wage but wages from different churches. Meaning a percent was set aside for him among the gentile church. For the work of ministry, for providence and for his family livelihood if he had had any.

2 Corinthians 11:8-10 KJV *I robbed other churches, taking wages of them, to do you service. And when I was present with you, and wanted, I was chargeable to no man: for that which was lacking to me the brethren which came from Macedonia supplied: and in all things I have kept myself from being burdensome unto you, and so will I keep myself. As the truth of Christ is in me, no man shall stop me of this boasting in the regions of Achaia.*

The above words simply means Paul had a pay incentive through all the churches he sate over among the gentiles. The ideal being, unlike the churches he started with which were authored by the desperation born of the persecution brought about by the death of Stephen; for those were Hebrews only Churches. Which he later left for a discourse with Barnabas to preach to the gentiles.

Acts 13:46-49 KJV *Then Paul and Barnabas waxed bold, and said, It was necessary that the word of God should first have been spoken to you: but seeing ye put it from you, and judge yourselves unworthy of everlasting life, lo, we turn to the Gentiles. For so hath the Lord commanded us, saying, I have set thee to be a light of the Gentiles, that thou shouldest be for salvation unto the ends of the earth. And when the Gentiles heard this, they were glad, and glorified the word of the Lord: and as many as were ordained to eternal life believed. And the word of the Lord was published throughout all the region.*

So, this tithe also was and is the portion of the pastoring team at branch level. Even as it was part of the Levite Israel over. It is the pastor's inheritance as Jesus a number of times underscored the ideal of man who will say he is following him. Or picking His call and still be inebriated in their birth rite family business or substance.

Matthew 19:16-26 KJV *And, behold, one came and said unto him, Good Master, what good thing shall I do, that I may have eternal life? And he said unto him, Why callest thou me good? there is none good but one, that is, God: but if thou wilt enter into life, keep the commandments. He saith unto him, Which? Jesus said, Thou shalt do no murder, Thou shalt not commit adultery, Thou shalt not steal, Thou shalt not bear false witness, Honour thy father and thy mother: and, Thou shalt love thy neighbour as thyself. The young man saith unto him, All these things have I kept from my youth up: what lack I yet? Jesus said unto him, If thou wilt be perfect, go and sell that thou hast, and give to the poor, and thou shalt have treasure in heaven: and come and follow me. But when the young man heard that saying, he went away sorrowful: for he had great possessions. Then said Jesus unto his disciples, Verily I say unto you, That a rich man shall hardly enter into the kingdom of heaven. And again I say unto you, It is easier for a camel to go through the eye of a needle, than for a rich man to enter into the kingdom of God. When his disciples heard it, they were exceedingly amazed, saying, Who then can be saved? But Jesus beheld them, and said unto them, With men this is impossible; but with God all things are possible.*

Luke 9:57-62 KJV *And it came to pass, that, as they went in the way, a certain man said unto him, Lord, I will follow thee whithersoever thou goest. And Jesus said unto him, Foxes have holes, and birds of the air have nests; but the Son of man hath not where to lay his head. And he said unto another, Follow me. But he said, Lord, suffer me first to go and bury my father. Jesus said unto him, Let the dead bury their dead: but go thou and preach the kingdom of God. And another also said, Lord, I will follow thee; but let me first go bid them farewell, which are at home at my house. And Jesus said unto him, No man, having put his hand to the plough, and looking back, is fit for the kingdom of God.*

The true nature of the call of God makes a man abandon shop and follow God. As did Peter, Matthew and the sons of Zebedee; they left all and followed Him. Even Matthew left the tax post and followed Him that instance. Meaning providence and everything should be Him if you indeed heard the call of God and did not just send self. A thing that many modern people rise to, that if they have substance and can sustain the church with their finance they do rise to the "call".

Matthew 9:9-11 KJV *And as Jesus passed forth from thence, he saw a man, named Matthew, sitting at the receipt of custom: and he saith unto him, Follow me. And he arose, and followed him. And it came to pass, as Jesus sat at meat in the house, behold, many publicans and sinners came and sat down with him and his disciples. And when the Pharisees saw it, they said unto his disciples, Why eateth your Master with publicans and sinners?*

Matthew 20:28-34 KJV *Even as the Son of man came not to be ministered unto, but to minister, and to give his life a ransom for many. And as they departed from Jericho, a great multitude followed him. And, behold, two blind men sitting by the way side, when they heard that Jesus passed by, cried out, saying, Have mercy on us, O Lord, thou Son of David. And the multitude rebuked them, because they should hold their peace: but they cried the more, saying, Have mercy on us, O Lord, thou Son of David. And Jesus stood still, and called them, and said, What will ye that I shall do unto you? They say unto him, Lord, that our eyes may be opened. So Jesus had compassion on them, and touched their eyes: and immediately their eyes received sight, and they followed him.*

If you have to provide for self and have to depend on self for the course of the work of God. It brings doubt to the call; if Christ says bring no staff or scrip of your own. Then it means He is ready to provide for His work of He sends you.

Matthew 10:9-10 KJV *Provide neither gold, nor silver, nor brass in your purses, Nor scrip for your journey, neither two coats, neither shoes, nor yet staves: for the workman is worthy of his meat.*

This is the tithe found in the book of **Numbers**;

Numbers 18:24-32 KJV *But the tithes of the children of Israel, which they offer as an heave offering unto the LORD, I have given to the Levites to inherit: therefore I have said unto them, Among the children of Israel they shall have no inheritance. And the LORD spake unto Moses, saying, Thus speak unto the Levites, and say unto them, When ye take of the children of Israel the tithes which I have given you from them for your inheritance, then ye shall offer up an heave offering of it for the LORD, even a tenth part of the tithe. And this your heave offering shall be reckoned unto you, as though it were the corn of the threshingfloor, and as the fulness of the winepress. Thus ye also shall offer an heave offering unto the LORD of all your tithes, which ye receive of the children of Israel; and ye shall give thereof the LORD'S heave offering to Aaron the priest. Out of all your gifts ye shall offer every heave offering of the LORD, of all the best thereof, even the hallowed part thereof out of it. Therefore thou shalt say unto them, When ye have heaved the best thereof from it, then it shall be counted unto the Levites as the increase of the threshingfloor, and as the increase of the winepress. And ye shall eat it in every place, ye and your households: for it is your reward for your service in the tabernacle of the congregation. And ye shall bear no sin by reason of it, when ye have heaved from it the best of it: neither shall ye pollute the holy things of the children of Israel, lest ye die.*

Like all other tithes, its redemption is found in the book of **Leviticus** in case of a owing or need to redeem any accrual.

Leviticus 27:30-31 KJV *And all the tithe of the land, whether of the seed of the land, or of the fruit of the tree, is the LORD'S: it is holy unto the LORD. And if a man will at all redeem ought of his tithes, he shall add thereto the fifth part thereof.*

The Second Tithe

The second tithe simply put is always called the tithe of the kraal or the festival Tithe. It is because within it is the offerings of mostly first things of the kraal. It is not a tithe to the Levite or the pastor of the moment but a self indulgence savings scheme meant to facilitate pilgrimages to Jerusalem and other parts of key areas of meeting places for the congregation of God.

One sure thing is to say; this tithe is no longer practical nor exacted by the child of God.

It was the savings; which were a second tenth of all things dedicated to be used by one who set them aside and their family. It was meant to be that annual holiday outing savings for the congregants. In simple terms: God required of Israel to appear before Him in Jerusalem three times a year and He did sort out a providence for the travel and the festivities of those three travels. They were holidays in a year and they had to have a way to do facilitate without failure.

In simple terms; God did not just instruct Israel to continually appear before Him but provided a system that would enable them to.

This is the form of tithing that we find in the book of **Deuteronomy**. Introducing a second tithe to Israel; a tithe they would spend on self in a church festival in Jerusalem. Not as a due to the priest or the Levite but a due to self. It was designed and made to make sure Israel reached the designated headquarters or place where it should be partaken of and the manner in which it was partaken was unreserved and open for it was for the one who gathered it to be festive and in holiday mood. Unlike the first tithe it is not the portion of the Lord; but the portion of increase as it was supposed to be brought year by year for the yield and increase of the field to prosper;

Deuteronomy 12:4-14 KJV *Ye shall not do so unto the LORD your God. But unto the place which the LORD your God shall choose out of all your tribes to put his name there, even unto his habitation shall ye seek, and thither thou shalt come: And thither ye shall bring your burnt offerings, and your sacrifices, and your tithes, and heave offerings of your hand, and your vows, and your freewill offerings, and the firstlings of your herds and of your flocks: And there ye shall eat before the LORD your God, and ye shall rejoice in all that ye put your hand unto, ye and your households, wherein the LORD thy God hath blessed thee. Ye shall not do after all the things that we do here this day, every man whatsoever is right in his own eyes. For ye are not as yet come to the rest and to the inheritance, which the LORD your God giveth you. But when ye go over Jordan, and dwell in the land which the LORD your God giveth you to inherit, and when he giveth you rest from all your enemies round about, so that ye dwell in safety; Then there shall be a place which the LORD your God shall choose to cause his name to dwell there; thither shall ye bring all that I command you; your burnt offerings, and your sacrifices, your tithes, and the heave offering of your hand, and all your choice vows which ye vow unto the LORD: And ye shall rejoice before the LORD your God, ye, and your sons, and your daughters, and your menservants, and your maidservants, and the Levite that is within your gates; forasmuch as he hath no part nor inheritance with you. Take heed to thyself that thou offer not thy burnt offerings in every place that thou seest: But in the place which the LORD shall choose in one of thy tribes, there thou shalt offer thy burnt offerings, and there thou shalt do all that I command thee.*

Deuteronomy 14:22-27 KJV *Thou shalt truly tithe all the increase of thy seed, that the field bringeth forth year by year. And thou shalt eat before the LORD thy God, in the place which he shall choose to place his name there, the tithe of thy corn, of thy wine, and of thine oil, and the firstlings of thy herds and of thy flocks; that thou mayest learn to fear the LORD thy God always. And if the way be too long for thee, so that thou art not able to carry it; or if the place be too far from thee, which the LORD thy God shall choose to set his name there, when the LORD thy God hath blessed thee: Then shalt thou turn it into money, and bind up the money in thine hand, and shalt go unto the place which the LORD thy God shall choose: And thou shalt bestow that money for whatsoever thy soul lusteth after, for oxen, or for sheep, or for wine, or for strong drink,*

or for whatsoever thy soul desireth: and thou shalt eat there before the LORD thy God, and thou shalt rejoice, thou, and thine household, And the Levite that is within thy gates; thou shalt not forsake him; for he hath no part nor inheritance with thee.

The Third Tithe

Whenever the third tithe is mentioned people generally think it was exacted from the Levitical tithe but it is not so. This conversation is usually born of people thinking the pastors are over privileged in the current dispensation. This conversation is usually born of the ideal that a portion within what the pastors are being given belongs to the poor but it's not so.

And again I would reiterate: it is not so.

The pastoral tithe is not by any means supposed to be touched by the poor nor the widow nor fatherless nor the stranger. It solely for the pastoral use and as it is clearly narrated by the word of God. The only thing taken from a tithe is a tithe of tithes and it is given to the Setman. Then the remaining nine percent is dispersed as pay to the church workers; and they are entitled to eat it in their own courts or personal space.

Numbers 18:24-32 KJV *But the tithes of the children of Israel, which they offer as an heave offering unto the LORD, I have given to the Levites to inherit: therefore I have said unto them, Among the children of Israel they shall have no inheritance. And the LORD spake unto Moses, saying, Thus speak unto the Levites, and say unto them, When ye take of the children of Israel the tithes which I have given you from them for your inheritance, then ye shall offer up an heave offering of it for the LORD, even a tenth part of the tithe. And this your heave offering shall be reckoned unto you, as though it were the corn of the threshingfloor, and as the fulness of the winepress. Thus ye also shall offer an heave offering unto the LORD of all your tithes, which ye receive of the children of Israel; and ye shall give thereof the LORD'S heave offering to Aaron the priest. Out of all your gifts ye shall offer every heave offering of the LORD, of all the best thereof, even the hallowed part thereof out of it. Therefore thou shalt say unto them, When ye have heaved the best thereof from it, then it shall be counted unto the Levites as the increase of the threshingfloor, and as the increase of the winepress. And ye shall eat it in every place, ye and your households: for it is your reward for your service in the tabernacle of the congregation. And ye shall bear no sin by reason of it, when ye have heaved from it the best of it: neither shall ye pollute the holy things of the children of Israel, lest ye die.*

The above words talk about the pastoral tithe. The pastoral tithe has to be fully used by the pastoral members of the congregation. They are supposed to exhume the tithe of tithes from the pastoral tithe and the remainder is to be used by the pastoral only for their household use and for their providence.

This is the tithe that Israel did give as an additional tithe every three years. It was called the third tithe and it was not given to the Levite nor was it gathered to the church; it was rather laid at or within the gates of the giver so that any who is in need may partake of it. It is this tithe that was called also the tithe of the needy or the poor. For it was solely laid at the gate for those who are in need to partake of it.

As said before; the tithe of the needy or the poor was not an annual event but done triennially to sup the gleanings and the providence of the seventh year. In simple terms, the tithe of the poor is not the same tithe as the tithe collected by pastors. It was never and has never been gathered in to the church house. It was supposed to be left out there among the people so the needy may partake of it. So, the poor and the widow and the fatherless' tithe: and the pastoral tithe are two independent tithes that do not have a thing in common and they are not the only tithes that were exacted out of the congregation of Israel.

Yet the church do requite the laid aside tithe though they are not able to fully stand with the current system of things. Not because they actually want the care of the poor to be met but to apportion the part given to the pastors. It all goes the way of Judas; to rob the tithe of the due received as Judas did want to rob Christ of the savor of the lady's perfume.

Mark 14:3-11 KJV *And being in Bethany in the house of Simon the leper, as he sat at meat, there came a woman having an alabaster box of ointment of spikenard very precious; and she brake the box, and poured it on his head. And there were some that had indignation within themselves, and said, Why was this waste of the ointment made? For it might have been sold for more than three hundred pence, and have been given to the poor. And they murmured against her. And Jesus said, Let her alone; why trouble ye her? she hath wrought a good work on me. For ye have the poor with you always, and whensoever ye will ye may do them good: but me ye have not always. She hath done what she could: she is come aforehand to anoint my body to the burying. Verily I say unto you, Wheresoever this gospel shall be preached throughout the whole world, this also that she hath done shall be spoken of for a memorial of her. And Judas Iscariot, one of the twelve, went unto the chief priests, to betray him unto them. And when they heard it, they were glad, and promised to give him money. And he sought how he might conveniently betray him.*

John 12:3-8 KJV *Then took Mary a pound of ointment of spikenard, very costly, and anointed the feet of Jesus, and wiped his feet with her hair: and the house was filled with the odour of the ointment. Then saith one of his disciples, Judas Iscariot, Simon's son, which should betray him, Why was not this ointment sold for three hundred pence, and given to the poor? This he said, not that he cared for the poor; but because he was a thief, and had the bag, and bare what was put therein. Then said Jesus, Let her alone: against the day of my burying hath she kept this. For the poor always ye have with you; but me ye have not always.*

It was indignation not apathy.

The Holy Bible says for he carried the bag of money and he would often help himself of it. Beware who handles the portion of the church worker; it might end up causing them to compare it with their worldly pay. A thing that will cause a riot within and a bit of envying to jealousy.

Ignorance is telling them the pastor is over exacting and taking the portion of the poor; a thing that is not so. Yet the church's burden has been reduced by abolishing the two other tithes that were exacted from the congregation of Israel. A thing that means the tithe of pilgrims and the tithe of the needy which are an extra twenty percent that was charged to Israel but not chargeable to the church.

Even though the Levite is mentioned to not be forgotten when it comes to the third tithe; the has to come out and get it from the saints' houses. There was no specific portion for the Levite in it, they just had to pick from the street from any.

Deuteronomy 14:28-29 KJV *At the end of three years thou shalt bring forth all the tithe of thine increase the same year, and shalt lay it up within thy gates: And the Levite, (because he hath no part nor inheritance with thee,) and the stranger, and the fatherless, and the widow, which are within thy gates, shall come, and shall eat and be satisfied; that the LORD thy God may bless thee in all the work of thine hand which thou doest.*

The immediate command after the command to do it triennially reads thus; *and shalt lay it up within thy gates: And the Levite, (because he hath no part nor inheritance with thee,) and the stranger, and the fatherless, and the widow, which are within thy gates, shall come, and shall eat and be satisfied; that the LORD thy God may bless thee in all the work of thine hand which thou doest.* The ideal to the third tithe being abolished means a reduction to the burdens of the church. As it was expected as the Levitical Tithe as an additional tithe not a subtraction from the two former tithes. A thing that means the thirty percent that was exacted from Israel has been reduced to a mare ten percent.

The Tithe For The Poor, The Needy And the Fatherless And The Stranger

Deuteronomy 14:28-29 KJV *At the end of three years thou shalt bring forth all the tithe of thine increase the same year, and shalt lay it up within thy gates: And the Levite, (because he hath no part nor inheritance with thee,) and the stranger, and the fatherless, and the widow, which are within thy gates, shall come, and shall eat and be satisfied; that the LORD thy God may bless thee in all the work of thine hand which thou doest.*

As Israel had to go the way of festivity three times a year; every third year they had to set aside a tithe. A tithe for the poor and the needy. As they were required to annually leave some gleanings behind for the poor among them. They were also required every third year to gather a tithe of all things for the poor by leaving it within their gates. A thing that would make it their village or city effort. Not an effort of Israel together but as per their inherent city or village.

With All Said And Done

This should be the point where one should say I am well enlightened about dues. With all said and done, it is time to say that is the complete thesis on the principle of dues. A due connotation as it took a be wilding sweep of scapes to sum the word tithe and its chronicles in order.

This coverage of the whole thesis of dues is not lacking but does not take time indwell the processes like how they are presented and separated. One such tithe being the tithe of the kraal and the presentation of firstlings from the kraal. Such things one can further study on their own as they are processes rather than groupings of tithes.

The other ideal is the transition from the agrarian tithe to the money tithe. It is a transition that took a long and vast time with silent years between. The silent years are so severe that even Israel or Jews of now do not pay the tithes that Jews in the old did pay. Since they no longer have the abiding common temple where their festival tithes and the three other pilgrimages should spend and be gathered for, for festivities. A thing that means also the laying of a tithe at the gate is currently impossible.

The many highs and lows that happened to Israel means; tithe is now a thing held on to and only enforced in the Christian church. Though not totally desolate; they rather have developed funding means rather than the ways they originally did it. So one would say it is up to the Christian to hold on to the button as they picked it. The single tithe is to say there was a way before Christianity that kept the congregation of God fully self sustainable. Meaning the church in its perfection should be a self sufficient organism. Living and growing within the means provided by God to sustain and maintain it to the day of harvest.

    Amen!

The Questionnaire

Tithe: The Complete Thesis Questions

Section A

In this section you are to either agree or dis agree with short statements by circle the correct answer; whether true or false. Where you have circled neither true or false it shall be concluded as and marked as wrong. Not deducting nor increasing your score/ marks. (30 minutes-30 marks)

1. Apostle Paul did not get paid by the church.

A. True
B. False

1. Shakespeare paid tithe.

A. True
B. False

1. The three tithes system is a Judaism only system of tithing.

A. True
B. False

1. Women did not pay tithe.

A. True
B. False

1. If the pastor or church work keeps another job other than in the house of God they should pay tithe.

A. True
B. False

1. Tithing is not compulsory but a choice one may not choose.

A. True
B. False

1. The current church must pay three tithes.

A. True
B. False

1. Abraham paid tithe.

A. True

B. False

1. Jacob paid tithe.

A. True
B. False

1. The church took care of Jesus out of its substance.

A. True
B. False

1. Tithe is no longer exacted in the church.

A. True
B. False

1. Israel collected a specific tithe for the needy among them.

A. True
B. False

1. Peter and the apostles collected wholesome funds from those who sold their fields instead of a tithe.

A. True
B. False

1. Those who work at the altar are not supposed to partake of the things of the altar.

A. True
B. False

1. The worker for God should engage their substance and livelihood to serve to God permanently.

A. True
B. False

1. Those who serve God should rely on the work to provide as the workman is worthy of his meat.

A. True
B. False

1. The tithe is a portion holy unto God.

A. True
B. False

1. It is acceptable to purchase anything with your tithe and bring it church as long as it is bought with a reconcilable amount.

   A. True
   B. False

1. A tithe is someone else' pay and you must bring timely to help them support their household.

   A. True
   B. False

1. The third tithe is still applicable in the church today.

   A. True
   B. False

1. The tithe of tithes of the second tithe was for Aaron the priest.

   A. True
   B. False

1. Nine Percent of the third tithe was for the Levites.

   A. True
   B. False

1. Aaron collected tithe.

   A. True
   B. False

1. Moses partook of the tithe.

   A. True
   B. False

1. Dues were abolished with the Law.

   A. True
   B. False

1. Tithe is an optional gift that any man can give to church.

   A. True
   B. False

1. Sowing seeds is how pastors are supposed to be paid.

   A. True
   B. False

1. Jesus spoke against tithing.

   A. True
   B. False

1. The principle of seedtime and harvest began in Genesis.

   A. True
   B. False

1. The principle of seedtime and harvest will end with time.

   A. True
   B. False

Section B

Circle one correct answer per question as your choice answer. In case where none or more than one answer is circled, tit shall be marked as being wrong and it shall neither deduct nor increase your score/ marks. (30mins - 30marks)

1. What is tithe supposed to be used for in church?

   A. To buy sound system
   B. To pay church bills
   C. To pay the pastor and church workers
   D. To support evangelism effort

1. Which of the language does the word tithe originate from?

   A. English
   B. Egyptian
   C. Latin
   D. Greek

1. Who did a schedule of dedication of the building of the church in Bethel?

   A. Abraham
   B. King David
   C. King Solomon
   D. Sarah

1. Why did Israel need the second tithe?

- A. Pay the Levite
- B. For pilgrims and feasting
- C. For feeding the poor among them
- D. To support the work of God

1. In the original seedtime and harvest principle; man was given what to sow back in to the soil?

- A. Seed
- B. Money
- C. Food
- D. Life

1. Where was the third tithe supposed to be gathered?

- A. At Jerusalem
- B. At the temple
- C. Within their gates
- D. By the Levites

1. What started the three tithe system?

- A. Judaism
- B. Christianity
- C. Aaron
- D. Jesus

1. What ended the three tithe system?

- A. The cross
- B. Judaism
- C. The apostles
- D. The prophets

1. Who paid tithe 430 years before the Law?

- A. Israel
- B. Melchisedek
- C. Abraham
- D. Joshua

1. Who provided for Jesus out of their substance during His crusades?

- A. The brethren
- B. The synagogue
- C. Himself

D. The twelve apostles

1. Who was created first: the man or his wife?

A. Behemoth
B. Wife
C. Leviathan
D. Man

1. What was Adam and Eve given to sow back in to the soil?

A. Apple seed
B. Tree of life
C. Fruits and herbs with seed
D. Fruits and herbs without seed

1. When will the principle of seedtime and harvest stop?

A. At the end of time
B. As long as the sun rise and set
C. At the end of the system of things as we know them
D. After the rapture

1. What did Jesus say a work man is worthy of?

A. Meat
B. Wages
C. Pay
D. Time

1. How many tithes did Israel pay?

A. One
B. Four
C. Three
D. Two

1. What is the tithe for the needy called?

A. The first tithe
B. The fourth tithe
C. The third tithe
D. Tithe of tithes

1. Which part of the dues is set aside for the Setman?

A. The third tithe
B. The Festival tithe
C. Tithe of tithes
D. Tithe

1. Who was supposed to use the second tithe?

A. The one who brings it
B. The Needy
C. The Church
D. The Levite

1. Who did Abraham pay his tithe to?

A. Jesus Christ
B. Melchisedek
C. Abimelech
D. Aaron

1. Who shall partake of the tree of life forever?

A. Everyone
B. The saints
C. Adam
D. Eve

1. Whose hire was the first tithe in Israel?

A. The Highpriest and the Levites
B. The Highpriest and Aaron
C. Melchisedek and Aaron
D. Melchisedek and the Levites

1. Whose substance did Abraham refuse take as a present?

A. The king of Gomorrah
B. The king of Israel
C. The king of Sodom
D. The king of kings

1. What did Paul say about his lack of exacting a wage from the church in Corinth?

A. He said he was robbing other churches to do them service
B. He said it I not good to exact a wage as a pastor
C. He said it is rude to exact wages as a pastor

D. None of the above

1. When was the tithe for the needy collected?

A. Triennially
B. Biannually
C. Every fourth year
D. Year by year

1. Who was Moses acting as to Aaron during Aaron's priesthood?

A. A brother
B. A friend
C. God
D. Sibling

1. God said He is making Moses as unto who to Pharaoh?

A. Master
B. Deliverer
C. God
D. Brother

1. What did Israel use for their feasting and pilgrimages?

A. The third tithe
B. The second tithe
C. The first tithe
D. Sowing seeds

1. Who was responsible for exacting tithe of tithes during the Law?

A. The Levites
B. The church board
C. Church elders
D. The congregation

1. How many percent did Israel pay in tithes every third year; when the tithe of the needy is being collected among other tithes?

A. 10%
B. 20%
C. 30%
D. 40%

1. Why do we still pay tithe?

A. God is still in the business of calling men to His work
B. To buy church equipment
C. To provide for church utilities
D. To help the needy

Section C

Pick any two titles below and write a whole leaf essay for each title: (1hr - 40marks)

1. First Tithe
2. Second Tithe
3. Third Tithe
4. The Principle of Seedtime and harvest
5. The three tithes of Judaism

Don't miss out!

Visit the website below and you can sign up to receive emails whenever Modise Tlharesagae publishes a new book. There's no charge and no obligation.

https://books2read.com/r/B-A-ERNM-TEBYF

BOOKS 2 READ

Connecting independent readers to independent writers.

Also by Modise Tlharesagae

Basic Realities Of Altars
The Marine Reality

Christian Doctrine
Anthropology
Baptismo
Creation
Thanatology
Eschatology
Angelology
Soteriology

Christian Principles
Cost Ethic
Order Ethic
Time Ethic
Good Ethic
Trust Ethic
Sate Ethic
Remit Ethic
Yonder Ethic
Dues Ethic

ESTABLISHING SERIES
Time: An Introductory Thesis
Prophecy: An Introductory Thesis
The Empty Office
Dues Ethic

Growers Series
Sabbath: The Basic Version
Man
The Collateral Power of Destiny
Dealing with Idols
Confess It
The Now Word
Stonewall
The Character of Sin

Introduction To Altars
An Introductory Thesis
Approaching Altars
Servicing Altars

Leadership Development
Soul Winning
Christian Counseling; The Work
The Empty Office
Order Ethic
Dues Ethic
Eschatology

Matrimonial Series
The Marriage: The Wedding

Pastoral Resources/ Theologian
Eschatos Logos
The Empty Office
Dues Ethic
Ministry of the Holy Spirit

Starter Series
Holy Spirit

The Total Man[1]
Edges of the Sword

Theologian/ Extra Curricular
Tithe; The Complete Thesis

Standalone
Sonship of Christ
The Empty Office
The Four Witnesses
Mark of Greatness
The Engrafted Word
Prayer
Kingdoms And Dominions
Interpreting Scripture
Nailing The Word
Tithe of Tithes
The Second And Third Tithe